COMMUNICATING
WITH MICROCOMPUTERS

Computers and People Series

Edited by

B.R. GAINES

The series is concerned with all aspects of man-computer relationships, including interaction, interfacing, modelling and artificial intelligence. Books are inter-disciplinary, communicating results derived in one area of study to workers in another. Applied, experimental, theoretical and tutorial studies are included.

COMMUNICATING WITH MICROCOMPUTERS

An introduction to the
technology of
man-computer communication

IAN H. WITTEN

Man-Machine Systems Laboratory
Department of Electrical Engineering Science
University of Essex, Colchester, U.K.

1980

ACADEMIC PRESS
A Subsidiary of Harcourt Brace Jovanovich, Publishers
London New York Toronto Sydney San Francisco

ACADEMIC PRESS INC. (LONDON) LTD.
24/28 Oval Road,
London NW1

United States Edition published by
ACADEMIC PRESS INC.
111 Fifth Avenue
New York, New York 10003

British Library Cataloguing in Publication Data
Witten, I H
    Communicating with microcomputers. – (Computers
    and people).
    1. Microcomputers
    2. Computer input-output equipment
    I. Title   II. Series
    001.6'44   QA76.5   80-40650
    ISBN 0-12-760750-1
    ISBN 0-12-760752-8 Pbk

Printed in Great Britain by
Whitstable Litho Ltd., Whitstable, Kent

Preface

The microprocessor revolution has given us new power to
handle information in almost every walk of life, and
effective techniques of man-computer interaction are
essential if this power is to be exploited for the benefit of
ordinary people. Information processing is now virtually
free. It is communication — both within a microcomputer
system and between it and the world outside — that
constrains applications. If machines cannot interact with
ordinary people in ways with which they feel at ease,
computers will remain the province of a technological
priesthood and continue to be treated with suspicion by
everyone else. If they can, the enormous potential of
computers to aid and enhance our lives will be made available
to all.

   This book introduces the non-specialist to the technology
of communicating with microcomputers. By placing particular
emphasis on low-cost techniques associated with small systems
and personal computers, the reader's attention is focussed on
the positive nature of the microprocessor revolution — how
machines can help people — rather than the negative aspects
which have received much publicity in the non-technical
press.

   With computers, as with all complex and extensive
subjects, it is difficult to know where to start. The book
begins by considering communication within the computer
system itself — the representation of information in
electrical form and the data paths which carry it from one
subsystem to another. The concepts of synchronization, of
contention, of central and distributed control, and of
addressing range emerge quite naturally from this approach.

We carefully steer away from the issue of programming, preferring not to treat it at all than to treat it cursorily and inadequately — there are many texts on the subject. Anyway, programming is not central to the study of man-computer communication channels, although it is certainly necessary for their implementation. The processor is treated as just another subsystem like the store or the interfaces to external devices: its role is played down quite deliberately in accordance with its new diminished status as a single, cheap, integrated circuit. The central component of a computer system from our viewpoint is the communication protocol, which appropriately enough is a logical construct rather than a piece of software or hardware.

Proceeding from communication within the computer system to communicating with the world outside, we find that the most important media for both input and output are light and electrical signals (which can be directly converted to sound waves or other mechanical effects). The principles of a variety of low-level interfaces are described: switches, keyboards, lights, various kinds of display, optical detection, analogue-to-digital and digital-to-analogue conversion, serial line interfaces. It is of great advantage to have already studied the means of communication within the computer system in the previous chapter, for the most mystifying part of commercial interface devices is the inward-looking rather than the outward-looking part.

The communication media of light and sound are treated extensively from a higher-level point of view, as graphics and speech. It is easy to justify concentration on graphics as a man-computer communication channel, for we are all familiar with its applications in amusement arcades and television games, and are beginning to see more serious uses in teletext and viewdata (the Post Office's Prestel). Computer speech is less common, more esoteric — despite the predominance of speech in everyday human communication. It is my belief, however, that speech systems are poised for take-off, and the next year or two will see a terrific explosion of them. We already have speaking toys, speaking language translators, reading machines for the blind — although they are rare. One frequently sees announcements in the technical press of devices such as typewriter attachments that let blind people check their work using speech, voice-operated domestic television controllers, and new continuous speech recognition systems on the market. Cheap speech synthesizers for computer hobbyists are manufactured in both Britain and the USA. Computer speech is losing its mystique — and this book will help.

The level of the book is suitable for the layman with some acquaintance with electronics. A tutorial glossary at the end of Chapter 1 serves to refresh the reader's memory of simple technical terms and electronic devices.

Ian H Witten
May 1980

Acknowledgements

I would like to thank the many friends and colleagues who
have helped me not just in writing this book but in
developing an appreciation of the importance and range of
man-computer studies. Brian Gaines and David Hill have been
especially influential in promoting awareness of the various
communication channels, and Chris Corbett, Pete Madams and
Steve Matheson have educated me in the hardware of computer
buses and interfaces. Dorinda Bath, Angie Corbett, and Paul
Griffith have worked with me on aspects of speech
communication, and many of my ideas on this subject derive
from fascinating conversations with Walter Lawrence. Phil
McCrea helped to design the structure of the book, and
constructive suggestions on improving the text have come from
Bruce Anderson, Rod Cuff, and John Foster. Kel Fidler,
Graham Long, and Peter Noakes have helped me in debugging my
ideas.

Margaret Swanson ably typed much of the book, and it was
set on a PDP-11/45 computer and printed using a Diablo
printer. Mike Sansom drew the pictures, and the Essex
Electronics Centre kindly loaned equipment for most of the
photographs in Chapter 1. I would like to thank City
Computer Systems for Figure 4.1, Dr Ian Benest for Figure
4.3, Monotype International for Figure 4.5, and Quest
Automation for Figure 4.28.

Permission to reproduce the following material is
gratefully acknowledged: Figure 4.20 from Texas Instruments,
"The Memory and Microprocessor Data Book", p 92; Appendix to
Chapter 3 from Motorola, "M6800 Microcomputer System Design
Data", pp 39-48; and Figures 5.10 and 5.11 from the Joint
Speech Research Unit (Crown Copyright reserved).

To Pam and Anna . . . and **the** new one

Contents

Computers and Communication

Computers are moving out of the private and impersonal
security of the air-conditioned computer room into the field.

> Day and night a small perspex box sits in a field in a
> remote part of Suffolk. Every fifteen minutes it
> wakes up, checks the air temperature and the light
> level falling on nearby plants, starts a cassette tape
> recorder and records the data, and goes back to sleep.
> Ecologists are using it to measure climatic variations
> to investigate the rate of photosynthesis by plants.

They are coming down-market, from the banks and oil companies
to the toybox.

> Five-year-old Anna has a new toy. In a clearly-
> recognizable voice it asks her to spell a word and she
> types it on the keyboard. When she gets it wrong, it
> tells her and gives her one more try. Sometimes she
> doesn't understand the word, so she presses a "repeat"
> key to hear it again. After ten words, she is told
> her score and starts again with a different list of
> words. The toy can do other things too, like play
> word guessing games. Of course, it isn't perfect.
> Educationally, it may even be undesirable, for when
> the words come out on the lighted display the letters
> are clumsy and all in capitals. Sometimes she still
> can't understand a word after several repeats. But
> she's fascinated, and will play for hours more.

Figure 1.1 Microcomputer in a field

Figure 1.2 Speak 'n Spell toy

Now machines help people to communicate with other people —

Young Barry is autistic — he refuses to communicate
with people. He too has just been given a new toy —
a little grey box. He picks it up, chews at it, and
tries to balance it on a joystick which sticks out the
top. By chance he touches two shiny buttons on the
side and it makes a noise like a whisper. He's
intrigued. Eventually he discovers that if you move
the joystick while pressing another pair of buttons it
makes speech-like noises — inarticulate, drunken-
sounding, but definitely human. He looks at his
teacher sitting beside him and smiles — an exciting

gift for her because he usually avoids eye-contact.
Later on he finds a lever on the side of the box,
which makes the voice high or low. But he can't
operate it together with the joystick, for that needs
three hands. It is rare for him to solicit assistance
from someone else; but he gestures to the teacher to
help. Now they have something to share.

— and machines to communicate with machines.

When trucks drive off the car ferry at Harwich, they
used to stop to be weighed and measured, for road
taxes depend in a complicated way on the size of the
vehicle.   Now   they   drive   straight across the
weighbridge, and two electronic eyes a couple of
metres apart watch their profile as they go past and
calculate from it their length. Easy? — no, for
truck drivers are canny and accelerate and decelerate
past the eye to try to fool it. But it isn't fooled,
for the profiles seen by the two watchers differ
slightly when speed changes occur and the device knows
how to compensate for them.

What is happening? Everyone has heard of the
"microprocessor revolution", the "computer on a chip". But
the change is not just one of size, or even of cost. The
kind of uses to which computers are put are changing too. To
compute means to calculate, reckon, count. That is what
computers were originally designed for — to solve
mathematical problems by number-crunching at super-human
speed. In the late 1940's the Government set up a committee
to decide how many computers Britain needed. It came up with
an answer — five! They hadn't reckoned on the field, the
toybox, the hospital, shop, factory, office, the home.
Nowadays, computers are better thought of as information-
processing machines rather than as number-crunchers. And as
the whole point of information is that it should be
communicated, the purpose of the processing is to communicate
it in a different form. This way we see computers in their
modern role of facilitating the communication of information.
This is not to say that number-crunching has disappeared:
mathematical problems still have to be solved, but they
assume less importance now because of the far greater volume
of communication-enhancing applications. The new role has
dwarfed, not ousted, the old. In the four vignettes above,

which incidentally are all taken from real life, only two of
the machines — the speaking toy and the truck measurer — do
a significant amount of calculation. And, curiously enough,
for the speech toy the vast bulk of the calculations are for
the purpose of decoding stored speech, not keeping score.

Let's not over-glorify this new role of machines. The
result of more effective communication of information can be
good or bad.

> Cindy's job is to pick substandard potatoes off a
> conveyer belt. She used to work in a big shed,
> standing by the belt with potatoes moving slowly past
> and picking up the mouldy and misshapen ones, throwing
> them into a bin. Now she has a desk in a nearby room
> with a TV set which shows the potatoes on the
> conveyer. Whenever she sees a bad one, she identifies
> it by pointing on the screen with a pen and the
> machine rejects it into the bin for her. Actually she
> prefers this change, for it was noisy and dirty in the
> shed compared with the peace of the office.   But she
> can't talk with the other girls as she used to — for
> there aren't any. The new system makes her so
> efficient that they are redundant.

And the new potential for information-gathering can be
intolerably intrusive, even sinister.

> At a checkout desk in a supermarket sits Dawn.   They
> have just replaced her old till with a new, electronic
> one. She prefers it because it's quieter and easier
> to operate; it's better for the management because the
> accounts and a tally of goods that have been sold are
> kept on a central computer, which all the tills
> communicate with. What Dawn doesn't know — yet — is
> that each entry she makes is monitored, timed, and
> recorded: at the end of the day her manager will be
> able to compare her speed and the number of mistakes
> she made with all the other checkout girls.

As usual, technology is neutral in the struggle between good
and evil. What it does is enhance the possibilities of both.
Barry's life has been changed for the better, Dawn's for the
worse. Cindy's is cleaner and quieter but her friends are
out of work; Anna's is more interesting — at least for the
next hour or so. This book is about the technology which

makes it all possible. It aims to spread understanding so
that people can appraise these new developments
intelligently, see the problems for themselves, and
participate in their solution.

Without recent advances in integrated circuit electronics
like the microprocessor, none of these devices would exist,
for they would all be impossibly expensive. However, the
techniques which facilitate communication between man and
machine, or between one machine and another, are all
independent of the microprocessor. Modern electronics is the
delivery van which brings them to the doorstep, not the goods
themselves. People who design the devices obviously need to
know about microprocessors and about programming. But the
principles and technology behind communication are really
much more important, for these, and not raw processing, are
the limiting factor in most applications. The major creative
step is the conception of the device rather than its design
and implementation, and for this an understanding of the
potential of the various communication methods is vital.

To begin, however, I must give you some idea of what
microprocessors are and why they are having such a great
impact upon society and upon industry.

MICROPROCESSORS

A microprocessor is a device that follows a plan. The
plan can be anything you like, provided it can be specified
exactly as a sequence of steps. People often think of
microprocessors as performing arithmetic, like a pocket
calculator. So they can, of course, since arithmetic
operations can be represented as plans — think of the
procedure for addition, or long division. But there are
plenty of other kinds of plan. Simply counting events can be
expressed as a plan. Or triggering an alarm when certain
conditions are met (the conditions must be stated precisely,
like "temperature greater than 80 C, rather than "dangerously
hot"). Or dialling telephone digits. Or associating a list
of telephone numbers with names. Or grading potatoes,
knitting, timing heart-beats.

A microprocessor can do any information-processing task
that can be expressed, precisely, as a plan. It is totally
uncommitted as to what its plan will be. It is a truly
general-purpose information-processing device. The plan
which it is to execute — which will, in other words, control
its operation — is stored electronically. This is the
principle of "stored program control". Without a program the

microprocessor can do nothing. With one, it can do anything. (Anything, that is, that can be specified as a plan. Some things, like recognizing places or faces from pictures, cannot . . . yet — although Cruise missiles do recognize target terrain from a stored map.)

The way you have to formulate a plan for a microprocessor is quite different from how you would do it for a person. If my wife asks me to turn up the central heating, she is specifying the intended result of my action rather than the way I should go about it — the communication is goal-directed. A microprocessor's plan must, in contrast, be procedure-directed; taking the form of a program of instructions to be executed to accomplish the result. It is no good saying "go into the kitchen and turn the knob on the wall 3 degrees clockwise" — which route should be taken? — what if the door is closed? — which wall? — where on the wall? The program must be expressed in miniscule steps of detail. To get a microprocessor to do something, we must ourselves know how to do it, in detail. This is why it can't recognize faces — although we can, we don't know how.

Furthermore, microprocessors can only perform information-processing tasks. To take action on the outside world, or to receive signals from it, a connection must be provided between the microprocessor's representation of information (as digital electronic signals) and the real-world representation — like dots of light on a display screen, or a musical note, or the motion of knitting needles. Such a connection between information representations is called an "interface". We will have more to say about interfaces later.

THE ECONOMICS OF INFORMATION PROCESSING

The important laws that govern microprocessors and related integrated circuit devices are laws of economics rather than laws of electronics. Let us summarize them.

1. Microprocessors are cheap because they are general-purpose and their development costs are shared between many users.
2. Microprocessor-based products are expensive to specify and develop because a microprocessor is a general-purpose, uncommitted device, and gives no clue to how it should be used.
3. While hardware always costs money, software — the program — is (almost) free to copy, once it has been developed.

Consider the first law — a microprocessor is cheap because it is general-purpose. Microprocessors cost only a few pounds. The raw material is insignificant — a chip of silicon, a plastic pack, some metal legs. You pay for organisation, for testing, for quality control, for distribution. Yet the development of a microprocessor — including design, chip development, generation of test procedures, setting up a production line — is enormously expensive. It is precisely because the final product is totally uncommitted as to how it is to be used that it is cheap — sales are high and the development cost is shared amongst millions of users. Microprocessors are the perfect example of mass-market economics.

For example, one popular microprocessor, the Motorola 6800, which was introduced in 1974, is currently selling around 200,000 a year and is priced at 5 - 10 pounds. The development cost was extremely high and difficult to estimate because of the novelty of large-scale integrated circuit technology in 1974. To make a device of similar complexity nowadays, provided that its function was completely specified in advance, would cost in the region of 200,000 pounds. It is only through sharing this development cost amongst a large number of purchasers that the individual chip price is so low. What makes sharing possible is the uncommitted nature of the device.

The net result is that information-processing hardware is virtually free.

The drawback comes with the second law. Microprocessor-based product design is costly because microprocessors are general-purpose. I have stressed that a microprocessor gives no indication of how it is to be used. It offers the peculiar feature of _deferred_ _design_, in that design of a microprocessor-based application is deferred until after the processor itself has been manufactured. The design is, to a very large extent, the program or plan. Because the microprocessor is so general-purpose, the designer has a new problem. Instead of building up the product design from elementary components, he must consider how to strip down the limitless possibilities afforded by the microprocessor, inhibiting its general-purpose, uncommitted nature to achieve the product he requires. This is a new task to the engineer, one of restricting possibilities rather than generating them. It's more like sculpture than Meccano! Coupled with this are the inevitable problems of a new, rapidly-developing, and complex technology.

Of course, in the ideal case when the product
characteristics are completely, unambiguously, and firmly
specified from the outset, the job is not difficult.
Usually, however, product specification and design tend to
proceed hand in hand — at least to some extent. With weak
project management this can lead to a microprocessor-based
disaster. Although it may seem easy to avoid, in fact
managers are often unaware of the virtually limitless
information-processing possibilities of microprocessors, and
as the project develops and their understanding increases,
they cannot resist the temptation to enhance the final
product.

The third law really accounts for the explosive growth in
the use of microprocessors. While the first two alter the
balance between hardware and development costs, the cost of a
prototype product is broadly comparable whether a
microprocessor is used or not — say to within an order of
magnitude. But once the prototype exists, laws 1 and 3
combine to make subsequent copies very cheap indeed.

Software is (almost) free to copy. There is a loose
analogy between the development of a microcomputer-based
system and the production of a recording of orchestral or
choral music, with a costly overhead of musicians,
rehearsals, and so on. It is expensive to make, but (almost)
free to copy. In fact copying software is cheaper than
copying audio tapes because it can be done at electronic
speeds while tape recorders are electromechanical devices
which cannot work quickly. Of course, easy copying of
software brings its own problem, namely, pirating.

The fact that software is free to copy leads to the maxim,
"let the microprocessor do the work". Software
implementation of a task may or may not incur a higher
development cost than hardware, but it will certainly be
cheaper in production.

HARDWARE BUILDING BLOCKS

At the centre of a microcomputer system is the
microprocessor chip itself. Usually the choice of processor
is not critical to the final unit — there are several,
similarly-priced, that could be used. What it does affect
seriously, however, is the product development process, and
there are strong reasons for conservatism in processor choice
because of the investment in experience and development
tools.

A microprocessor cannot operate without a program, and

Figure 1.3 Chips

this is held in a _store_. Further storage must be provided
for recording intermediate results of calculations and
changing quantities, like the profile in the truck measurer,
of the score in the speaking toy. The program storage,
however, should be relatively permanent and non-volatile so
that it cannot be corrupted and remains even when power to
the unit is switched off. Such storage is called ROM —
read-_only_ memory. Some method of entering the program into
the store in the first place is necessary: with ordinary ROM
this is done during manufacture. More convenient for
product development is PROM — _programmable_ read-only memory
— which permits once-and-for-all programming after
manufacture, using a special device called a PROM-programmer
or (colloquially) PROM-blaster. Even more convenient is
EPROM — _erasable_ programmable read-only memory — which
allows the store to be erased, for example, by the
application of ultraviolet light, and subsequently reprogrammed.

The size of the program storage is naturally determined by
the size of the program. Most microprocessors organize store
into 8-bit chunks called "bytes", and bytes are counted in
units of 1024 (Kbytes) — these units are explained further
in the Appendix to this chapter. Typical microprocessor
programs occupy anything from 256 bytes to 8 Kbytes (8192
bytes).

Storage for the data which is processed by the
microcomputer system cannot be ROM, for it must be alterable
by program instructions. This kind of store is read-_write_
memory, called RAM. (RAM actually stands for "random-access"
memory, a misleading term — since ROM is just as "random-
access" — which is an unfortunate historical hangover from

pre-microprocessor days.) The size of RAM is determined by
the volume of data which must be retained by the processor.

As we saw above, ROM is not necessarily completely
unalterable, for in the case of EPROM the store can be erased
and reprogrammed. The important distinction between ROM and
RAM is that the latter can be altered by program
instructions, whereas the former cannot. Furthermore, RAM is
usually volatile in the sense that its contents disappear
when power is turned off, while ROM is more permanent. Note
that while we have read-only and read-write store, there is
no such thing as write-only store (except in jokes). (Why
not?)

The microcomputer is driven by a clock (see the Appendix
to this chapter) which synchronizes the various subsystems.
Clock speeds vary from 500 kHz to 10 MHz. The clock
determines the rate of execution of instructions by the
processor, which is usually in the region of 100000 to
1000000 instructions a second for present-day
microprocessors.

Assembling together all these components of a
microcomputer system, we have the microprocessor itself, some
ROM and RAM, interfaces to communicate with the outside
world, and a clock. How they are all connected together is
described in the chapters that follow. One of the paradoxes
of microcomputers is that the connections can cost more than
the chips themselves. Designing a hardware configuration for
a particular application is part of the process of completing
the design that was deferred when the components were built.
And since the cost of this is shared between the purchasers
of the application device only, and not between the vastly

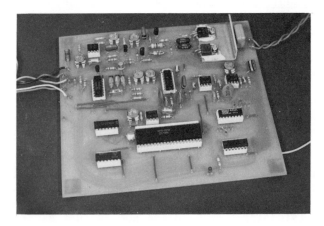

Figure 1.4 Chips mounted on a circuit board

greater numbers who buy the individual chips, it can account
for a substantial proportion of the device's price.

Other hardware building blocks for a microcomputer system
are the power supply, either battery- or mains-driven, the
box it goes in, and the mechanical keys and switches that are
needed to control it. While trivial from the point of view
of information-processing, these often account for a large
part of the cost of the finished device. By letting the
microprocessor do the work, designers eliminate switches and
knobs whenever possible, for this may result in worthwhile
savings and increased reliability. In this way the fact that
information-processing is now (virtually) free encourages
good human engineering: economic forces lead the designer to
consider what control is <u>really</u> necessary over the device and
deter him from adding bells and whistles.

PERIPHERALS

What's it like to use a computer system? In the bad old
days it was punched cards or paper tape for input, and
badly-printed upper-case-only output from a line printer.
You never saw the machine itself, which isn't necessarily a
bad thing, but more importantly you never interacted with it
on a reasonable time-scale. Jobs which you submitted were
returned hours or even days later, by which time the problem
had gone out of your head and you were thinking of other
things.

Now, microcomputers are so cheap that they can serve you
at your own convenience. More often than not you don't even

Figure 1.5 Box and power supply

know they're there, in your washing machine, sewing machine,
or car — except when you read the manufacturers'
advertisements! But suppose you have to develop a computer
program, or commission a new interface. Then you sit at a
television-style display with a typewriter keyboard, and
everything you type is interpreted by the machine
immediately. Programs and data are stored on a magnetic
disk, much like an ordinary record, which rotates
continuously inside its housing and is read and written by a
magnetic record/replay head under control of the processor.
Disks can hold from one to a hundred Mbytes of information —
enough for several books (this book contains about 250000
characters — 0.25 Mbyte). You can enter programs by just
typing them in, have them stored on the disk, and alter them
subsequently with a special "editor" program. A fast printer
sits beside the computer for producing "hard copy" at around
a line of text per second — for it is very difficult to work
on a program or piece of text without having it on paper.
Surprisingly, perhaps, the television display alone isn't
enough: it is no use for constant cross-referencing because
it only shows a couple of dozen lines at a time, and you
can't scribble on it!
    Most of your time while using the machine is spent
communicating with it, not computing (or rather, not waiting
while it does the computing). Your perception of the system
will probably be dominated by the communication channels at
your disposal rather than by the details of the processor
itself. Furthermore, most of its time is spent
communicating, too — with you, with the disk, with the
printer. Contrast this with the punched-card and paper-tape

Figure 1.6 A small microcomputer system

days: truly the microprocessor revolution is about
communication and not computation.

PLAN OF THE BOOK

This book is about communicating with microcomputers. The
emphasis is on _micro_ computers because new low-cost devices
for man-computer interaction, which are beginning to emerge
on the market, are highlighted at the expense of more
sophisticated equipment that is only suitable for large
computer installations.

The meaning of communication is taken rather broadly, and
to limit the size of the book while keeping the prerequisite
knowledge down to a minimum we delve deeply into just four
topics instead of attempting to cover everything. These
topics span an enormous range — from the hardware which
interconnects electronic subsystems, at the grainy detail of
transistor circuits, to the difficulty of English
pronunciation for speech synthesis from ordinary text. I
feel that it is important to have some appreciation of the
problems at all levels. The people we need most in
technology today are those who are capable of gliding easily
from one level of representation to another — from ideas on
man-machine interaction derived from psychology and
linguistics to details of microcomputer system design — and
not specialists who can only view the arena of technology
from one narrow perspective. But it would be wrong to
pretend that the result is a neatly integrated, uniform book.
In many ways it reads like a collection of weakly linked
monographs! The advantage for you, the reader, is that the
individual chapters can be read in isolation — if you find
that the early parts contain too much electronic detail, skip
them: it won't impair your understanding of later material
too much.

The first subject is how the components of a computer
system communicate between themselves. We are interested in
the logical structure of the communication rather than the
fine details of particular configurations. What directions
does information travel in, and how can communication be
designed to allow a reasonable degree of autonomy between
subsystems (to exploit their inherent parallelism) while
retaining control and avoiding contention? From the physical
point of view, connections are passive and uninteresting —
just bits of wire. But to make a system work a logical
superstructure of convention and protocol must be built and
adhered to by every subsystem. This is what makes the design

of an interconnection system interesting.

Having established the means of communication within the
computer system itself, we look at the mechanics of
communicating, or interfacing, with the outside world.
Interfaces connect on the one hand to the subsystems of the
computer, and on the other to real-world events of people,
light, sound, and motion. To connect to people we need
lights and switches, keyboards and displays, pens and TV
screens, speech synthesizers and recognizers. To receive
information from other machines we need transducers to
measure temperature and torque, smells and strain, pressure
and pollution; reduce them to electrical form; and convert
the resulting analogue signals to digital for the processor.
Although we cannot cover the instrumentation problems of
non-electrical variables, we do describe the method of
converting between analogue and digital representations, and
show how positional information can be obtained directly in
digital form by optical techniques. The fundamental logical
problems of synchronizing external events to a microcomputer
system are examined; and so are the means whereby an
interface can pre-empt the processor and communicate directly
with the other subsystems of the microcomputer.

Our third and fourth topics involve rather higher-level
interaction between people and machines using graphics and
speech. In both these areas the cost of hardware is
plummeting and new horizons are appearing. Interactive
graphics is interesting technically because if a complicated
picture has to change quickly and unobtrusively the computer
will not be fast enough to regenerate all the points in time
itself, and so some special hardware must be added. The
slogan "let the processor do the work" cannot be obeyed
because the processor isn't fast enough! Its capability for
executing hundreds of thousands of instructions a second is
not sufficient because the picture will contain tens or
hundreds of thousands of points, and each one must be
displayed many times a second to prevent the picture from
flickering. Until fairly recently, interactive computer
graphics was the province of the rich. When computers were
expensive and used only by a small group of professionals,
poor communication channels were tolerable, for the cost of
the labour needed to re-interpret printed results in the more
meaningful form of pictures and verbal reports was
insignificant in comparison with the cost of the equipment
itself. Now, cheap information-processing gives a tremendous
incentive to manufacturers to provide more suitable
communication tools. And the tree is bearing fruit!

We noted above that additional hardware must be added to

help the processor generate pictures quickly. This produces
a trade-off between equipment cost and graphics capability,
and the Graphics chapter is primarily devoted to exploring
the best compromises. It turns out, not surprisingly, that
knowledge of the types of pictures which are to be displayed
can sometimes be used to lower the cost — for example, if
only text is shown quite a cheap interactive display can be
made. We also examine some devices for graphical input —
the light-pen, which triggers at the precise time that a spot
of light appears under it on the screen, and a tablet which
uses electrical laws to determine the position of a stylus.

   Until recently, speech communication with computers was
not even the province of the rich — it just didn't exist.
Now you can buy the Speak 'n Spell toy from an ordinary
toyshop. In a sense, of course, it is only a development of
the tape recorder, with no moving parts, low power
consumption, and instant access to recorded segments.
However, the vast improvements in the technology of speech
recording and replay open up a multitude of new applications.
Besides covering speech storage, we examine speech synthesis
from textual representations, either phonetics or plain
English. Such systems are already being used by blind
people, although the speech quality is extremely poor. The
problems are ones of software, for speech synthesis hardware
is already being marketed cheaply, and we can expect to hear
a great deal more of synthetic speech in the near future.
The converse problem of speech recognition is not nearly so
far advanced, although some limited word recognizers are
being used commercially.

   At the end of each chapter appears a short appendix which
covers some aspect of the subject in more detail. These
appendices are slightly more difficult to read than the main
text, and can be skipped if desired. They are provided to
whet the interested reader's appetite for a more analytical
study of communicating with microcomputers than it is
possible to provide in an introductory, and practically-
oriented, book. The exception is the appendix to this
chapter, which contains a tutorial glossary designed to
introduce to you some terms and concepts which will be used
later.

FURTHER READING

Brooks, F.P (1975) "The Mythical Man-month." Addison-Wesley,
   Reading, Massachusetts.
        A readable and compelling account of the real

problems that face people who organize large
programming projects. Comments perceptively on
the pitfalls that confront the programmer, and
shows why software is never produced on schedule.
Completely non-technical.

Evans, C. (1979) "The Mighty Micro." Gollancz, London.
An optimistic, exciting, and almost racy account
of how microprocessors will affect the lives of
us all — sooner than you think!

Nelson, T. (1974) "Computer Lib." Ted Nelson, Publisher.
This is the counterculture computer book —
American, zany, packed with background
information, and fun to read, too.

Nelson, T. (1977) "The Home Computer Revolution." Ted
Nelson, Publisher.
"Computer screens on the kitchen table. Computer
screens by the bedside. Computer screens on the
office desk. Computer screens on automobile
dashboards, Coke machines, ticket dispensers ..."
A provocative and optimistic account of the role
of computers in the home of the future.

Ogdin, C.A. (1978) "Software Design for Microcomputers."
Prentice-Hall, Englewood Cliffs, New Jersey.
This is the best introduction to programming that
I know, emphasizing program design rather than
just program writing. Software is not discussed
at all in the present book. If you want to go
further into communicating with microcomputers,
you'll have to come to grips with it, and Ogdin's
book is the right way.

Osborne, A. (1976) "An Introduction to Microcomputers Volume
1 — Basic Concepts." Adam Osborne and Associates,
Berkeley.
Osborne describes the structure of the
microprocessor itself — what it looks like, how
it works, what it can do, how you write programs.
Again, this complements the present book, where
we are more concerned with communicating with the
processor than with detailing what it does.

APPENDIX: TUTORIAL GLOSSARY

This glossary explains some technical terms and concepts which are used in the rest of the book. It is in three sections: terminology, digital electronics, and analogue electronics; and the entries appear not in alphabetical order but as a tutorial sequence.
I have endeavoured to explain just what you need to know to follow the rest of the book, and no more. This means that some of the descriptions of devices fall very much short of the full story, and if you are at all familiar with the concepts already, don't bother to read on — you will almost certainly learn nothing from this over-simplified discussion.
If you aren't familiar with the concepts, the best way to use the glossary is to scan it quickly now and return to it whenever you need to, for more detail. The terminology part is used fairly constantly thoughout the rest of the book. Digital electronics is used quite a bit in Chapters 2 and 3, and it should not be hard to understand what the various devices do when you meet them as they are used and refer back to this glossary. The analogue electronics part may seem rather off-putting if you have little knowledge of electronics, but if you have trouble with it, don't despair — the sections which use it can be skipped without preventing you from understanding the rest of the book.

1. Terminology

Bit   (Contraction of "binary digit") A "bit" is a
             distinction between two states. It can be
             represented by a number which can have either of
             the values 0 and 1, or as the voltage on a wire
             being high (say, greater than 2 volts) or low
             (say, less than 0.8 volts), or as a door being
             open or closed, or your hat being on or off.
             The first two representations are really better
             than the last two for the purposes of this book.

Byte   Eight bits. For example,
                 01101010
             may represent the contents of a particular byte
             at a particular time.

Word   This is a string of binary digits which is
             treated by a computer as a single unit of data.
             Many computers have 8-bit words, and for these a

word is a byte. "Word" is a less specific term
than "byte".

Word length
The number of bits in a word (for example, there
are machines with word lengths of 4, 8, 12, 16,
18, 20, 24, and 32 bits).

Kbit   (Kilobit) 1024 bits. 1024 is chosen because it
is an exact power of 2, namely 2^{10}.

Kbyte   (Kilobyte) 1024 bytes.

Mbyte   (Megabyte) 2^{20} bytes (about a million).

msec   (Millisecond) 10^{-3} sec, ie a thousandth of a
second.

usec   (Microsecond) 10^{-6} sec, ie a millionth of a
second.

nsec   (Nanosecond) 10^{-9} sec.

Hz   (Hertz) Once a second. The second hand of a
clock rotates at 1/60 Hz, and the minute hand at
1/3600 Hz. A normal heart beats at slightly
greater than 1 Hz. The string of a piano
vibrates at around 260 Hz when middle C is
struck.

kHz   (Kilohertz) 10^3 Hz (a thousand times a second).

MHz   (Megahertz) 10^6 Hz (a million times a second).

Digital and analogue representation
You know the difference between a digital and an
analogue watch. The digital one measures time
in discrete steps while the analogue one's hands
move continuously (well, even an analogue watch
"ticks" and so could be considered by a purist
to be digital!). The essential distinction is
between a discrete and a continuous
representation — a voltage is continuous,
whereas a logic level (see below) is discrete.

2. Digital electronics

Logic level
A range of voltages which are considered to be
the same. When a binary digit is represented by
the voltage on a wire, a range of voltages is
specified which corresponds to the bit being in
one state, and another (non-overlapping) range
for the other state. A common specification is

$0 \leq$ voltage $\leq$ 0.8 — LOW logic level
$2 \leq$ voltage $\leq$ 5   — HIGH logic level

If the voltage falls between these ranges, its
logic level is undefined.

Positive logic
A LOW logic level is interpreted as a 0 and a
HIGH as a 1.

Negative logic
A LOW logic level is interpreted as a 1 and a
HIGH as a 0.

Inverter A device which changes a LOW logic level to a
HIGH one and vice versa. Figure 1.7 shows the
symbolic representation.

AND gate A 2-input device with one output which is HIGH
only when both the inputs are HIGH (Figure 1.8).

Flip-flop This is a device that has two different states,
let us say "0" and "1", and stays in whichever
state you put it. An ordinary domestic light-
switch is a mechanical flip-flop — a spring
ensures that the switch stays on when you turn
it on, and off when you turn it off.
One kind of flip-flop has two inputs, SET and
RESET (Figure 1.9(a)). When these are LOW, the
flip-flop does not change state. If SET goes to

input	output
LOW	HIGH
HIGH	LOW

Figure 1.7 Inverter

input1	input2	output
LOW	LOW	LOW
LOW	HIGH	LOW
HIGH	LOW	LOW
HIGH	HIGH	HIGH

Figure 1.8 AND gate

a HIGH logic level, then the flip-flop goes to
the "1" state and remains there even when the
SET input becomes LOW again. Only when RESET
becomes HIGH does it go to the "0" state, and
again it will remain there when the RESET input
goes LOW again.

Another type of flip-flop has a "clock" input
and one other input (Figure 1.9(b)). When CLOCK
goes HIGH, the flip-flop's state becomes "1" if
the other input is HIGH and "0" if it is LOW.
The output of the flip-flop does not change,
even if the input changes, until the next clock
"tick".

Clock   A device with no inputs and an output which
          changes regularly from one logic level to the
          other (Figure 1.10). Whether the output is a
          short pulse or just a change in logic level
          doesn't matter (for the purposes of this book).
          The important thing about a clock is its
          frequency (measured in kHz or MHz), or,
          equivalently, the "clock period" or interval
          between ticks (in msec or usec).

Register A register is a collection of flip-flops (often
          8 of them). An 8-bit register will have 8
          inputs, 8 outputs, and a single LOAD terminal
          (Figure 1.11). The LOAD line acts as a clock
          for each of the 8 inputs, so that they are all
          loaded together when it is activated.

Counter   A counter is a register with some logic attached
          which makes it count in binary. It has a CLEAR
          terminal (which sets the contents to 0 when
          activated), a COUNT terminal (which adds one to
          the contents), and several data outputs (Figure
          1.12).

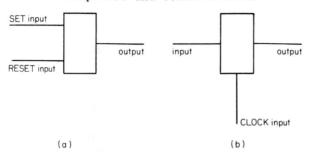

Figure 1.9 (a) Flip-flop with SET and RESET inputs
          (b) Flip-flop with a CLOCK input

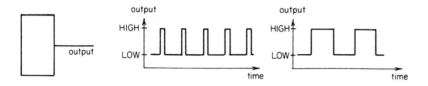

Figure 1.10 A clock, with two kinds of output waveform

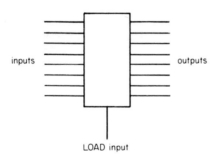

Figure 1.11 An 8-bit register

3. Analogue electronics

Voltage, current, resistor
          I assume you know what these are.

Ohm's law The current through a resistor is proportional
          to the voltage across it:
                V (voltage) = I (current) x R (resistance).

Vcc   Symbol used for power supply voltage (usually 5

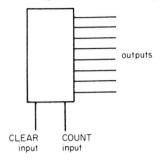

Figure 1.12 An 8-bit counter

or 12 volts in the circuits we will consider).
Historically, the "cc" stands for "common-
collector", because the collectors of
transistors were all connected to Vcc (see
below, under "transistor"). This is not always
the case in present-day circuits.

Ground   0 volts.

Diode   Device which allows current to pass in one
                direction only (see Figure 1.13).
                    Actually, if the diode is connected as in
                Figure 1.13(a), it will probably burn out,
                because there is nothing to limit the current
                through it. With no resistance, or in practice
                a very small resistance (for even wires have
                some resistance!), Ohm's law gives a very large
                current for any applied voltage.

Current-limiting resistor
                So when connecting a diode, we include a
                current-limiting resistor as in Figure 1.14.
                This controls the current that flows in the
                circuit.

Diode drop
                When current is flowing through a diode, the
                voltage at the two terminals is different. The
                diode itself makes the voltage drop. The size
                of this "diode drop" is about 0.7 volts. Thus
                to calculate the current flowing in the circuit
                of Figure 1.14, note that the lower terminal of
                the diode is grounded and so the upper one is at
                0.7 volts, and thus the voltage across the
                current-limiting resistor is Vcc - 0.7. Then

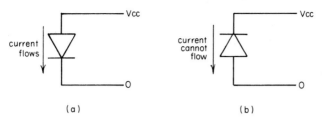

Figure 1.13 (a) A diode conducting current
            (b) A diode which cannot conduct current

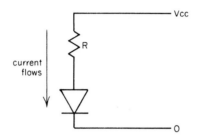

Figure 1.14 Conducting diode with current-limiting resistor

Ohm's law gives the value of the current for any
size of resistor.

Transistor

A transistor is an electronic switch, which uses
a current to switch another current on and off.
It has three terminals, called the base,
collector, and emitter. The input current flows
between the base and emitter, and the output
between the collector and emitter, as shown in
Figure 1.15.

To turn a transistor on, you make current
flow between the base and the emitter. Suppose
the emitter is connected to ground (0 V). Then
a positive voltage on the base will cause
current to flow, turning the transistor ON. If
the collector is connected to a positive voltage
as well (like the power supply Vcc), current
will flow between it and the emitter, since the
transistor is ON. A zero voltage on the base
will turn the transistor OFF, inhibiting the
collector-emitter current.

In practice, current-limiting resistors are

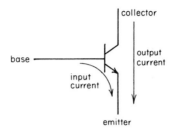

Figure 1.15 A transistor

needed at both the base and the collector, as in
the circuit of Figure 1.16. This circuit has a
voltage input and a voltage output. When the
input is HIGH, current flows between base and
emitter, turning the transistor ON and allowing
the collector-emitter current to flow. Thus the
output is LOW, because the collector and emitter
are effectively connected. (Actually, there is
a voltage drop involved here, and the collector
will be at about 0.2 V.) When the input is LOW,
the transistor is turned off and so the base and
emitter are effectively disconnected. Then the
output will be HIGH, for no current is flowing
through the collector resistor. The circuit
acts as a logic inverter.

In a practical circuit the output of Figure
1.16 will be connected to something else (for
example, to the base of another transistor
switch through a current-limiting resistor), and
the actual output voltage will depend on how
much current is drawn through the collector
resistor. Thus one device loads another by
drawing current from its output. When
interconnecting these circuits, care must be
taken to prevent loading from altering the
voltage so much as to change the logic level it
represents.

Comparator
A circuit which takes two voltages as input,
compares them, and outputs a HIGH logic level if
one is greater than the other and a LOW one if
it is less (Figure 1.17).

Operational amplifier
An "op amp" is a three-terminal device with two

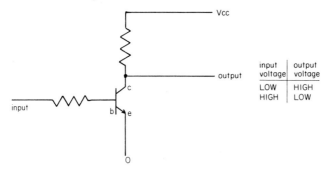

Figure 1.16 A transistor circuit

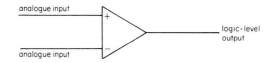

Figure 1.17 Comparator

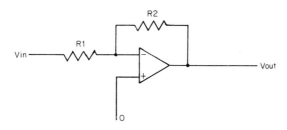

Figure 1.18 Circuit using an operational amplifier

inputs and one output. (Actually, the op amp
must be connected to a power supply as well,
making an extra two terminals.) The input is
differential — only the voltage difference
between the inputs is significant. The output
is the input voltage difference amplified by a
very large factor.

Because of its very large amplification, the
most common way to use an op amp is in a
feedback configuration with the output connected
back to the input — Figure 1.18 shows a typical
circuit. Then, the voltages in the circuit will

adjust themselves so that the differential input
is zero in the ideal case, although in practice
a small input difference will remain. So, in
the Figure, we assume that the "-" input is at
ground (0 V).

A further property of an (ideal) op amp is
that its input does not draw current from
whatever is connected to it. Thus the current
through R1, namely (Vin - 0)/R1, must equal that
through R2, (0 - Vout)/R2. Hence

$$\frac{Vin}{R1} = -\frac{Vout}{R2}, \quad \text{so} \quad Vout = -Vin\frac{R2}{R1}.$$

Computer Buses

The components of a computer system include a processing unit
(often a microprocessor chip), a store, and input-output
interfaces to enable it to communicate with the world
outside. How are these components to be connected together?
People often have a mental picture such as that of Figure
2.1, where the processor is at the centre and communicates
with the store on one side and input-output interfaces on the
other, and indeed this is the way that early computers were
constructed. However, it is apparent that in this
configuration the processor constitutes a bottleneck, for
usually the input-output data is placed into or taken out of
store rather than being processed immediately. This leads to
the inclusion of the dashed line in the figure, as a "direct
memory access" channel. And this is the way that early
minicomputers were built.

This kind of interconnection, where every device is
connected to every other, quickly becomes cumbersome as more
devices are added to the system. Recent minicomputers, and
almost all microprocessor systems, use the alternative
structure of Figure 2.2, where a common bus is used to
connect the various devices. "Bus" is a contraction of the

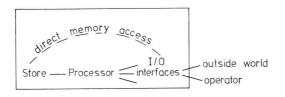

Figure 2.1 Processor-centred computer model

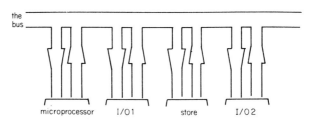

Figure 2.2 Bus-centred computer model

Latin "omnibus", which means "for all" — indicating that the
bus is used for all data transfers between subsystems.

It may seem that the bus structure has re-introduced the
bottleneck that we saw in the processor-centred computer
model, only now it is the bus and not the processor which is
responsible for the blockage. This is perfectly true.
However, the bus is such a simple device — just a bundle of
wires — that the bottleneck can be relieved by making data
transfers on it go very fast, whereas transfers through the
processor are much slower.

It is obviously important that more than one device should
not try to use the bus to transmit data at the same time. It
is, however, possible to imagine a single data transfer being
directed to many receiving devices at once — although
transfers along the bus should be received only by the
devices for which they are intended. If I/O device 1
transfers data to the store, for example, it should not be
received by I/O device 2 as well (or instead!). In practice
it is much easier for the sender to specify a unique
destination device for the data rather than a set of
recipients, and bus structures are designed for single-
destination transfers only.

Specifying the destination is usually accomplished by
dividing the bus into two parts: an <u>address bus</u> and a <u>data
bus</u>. A sending device puts the address of the intended
receiver on the address bus, and the data for it on the data
bus. Devices ensure that they only accept the data from the
bus when the address bus indicates that they are the intended
recipient. Addresses, like data, are simply binary numbers
with a specified number of bits. Typically, the address bus
is 16 bits wide and the data bus is 8 bits wide. This allows
for addressing up to 2^{16} = 65,536 different devices! There
is hardly likely to be this number of separate devices on the
bus, of course: the number is so large because some devices
— notably stores — often incorporate many different
addresses. A single store may easily contain 2^{15} = 32,768
separate locations, each of which is addressable individually

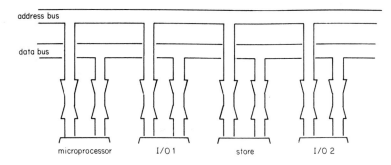

Figure 2.3 Address and data buses

on the bus. This store would use up half of the "address
space" of a 16-bit address bus.

A bus is simply a bundle of wires. The bus of Figure 2.2
is redrawn in Figure 2.4 to show the individual lines,
assuming that it is 4 bits wide. Notice that although two
channels are used in Figure 2.2 to show the information
coming off the bus separately from that going on to it, both
channels are implemented on the same piece of wire in Figure
2.4. The information on the wire is bi-directional.
Actually, the concept of the "direction" of a bus transfer
needs closer examination — in electrical terms the
information does not travel along the wire but appears
simultaneously (at the speed of light) all along its length
as the voltage on the wire changes. However, there is a
cause-and-effect relationship between the sending device and
the receiver which can usefully be thought of as the
"direction" of the transfer. Although the bus must carry
information in both directions, there is nothing special
about the wire itself — any piece of wire can be driven from
either end. It is the way that it is driven that makes it
bi-directional.

This chapter is about the technology of buses. We have
already seen fast buses, and bus lines (perhaps "conductors"
would be a better word). We will meet bus drivers, and see
how bus collisions can occur when more than one driver tries
to drive the same bus. Interestingly enough, collisions are
less likely when the bus is going fast! The next section
discusses how bus lines are driven. The bi-directional
nature of the lines makes ordinary TTL logic gates unsuitable
for putting information on to buses, and there are two
commonly-used alternative methods: open-collector gates and
tri-state gates. Next the problems of bus synchronization
are introduced and discussed. Generally, the various devices
on a bus are synchronized individually by local clocks, but

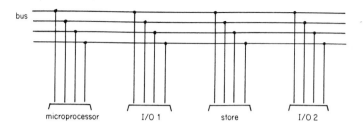

Figure 2.4 Individual lines of a 4-bit bus

they are not synchronized together by a common clock.
Finally, after a brief discussion of read and write control
on the bus, the difficult problem of bus contention is
described — what happens when two or more devices on a bus
simultaneously decide that they want to use it for
transmission?

DRIVING A BUS LINE

Failure of Ordinary TTL

Ordinary transistor-transistor logic (TTL) suffers from
the disadvantage that the outputs of two logic gates cannot
be connected together. Thus if two devices are connected to
the bus as in Figure 2.5, and each may at some time put a
signal on to it, ordinary TTL gates cannot be used to drive
the bus.
The reason is as follows. TTL gates can only output logic
0 or 1. Suppose that device 2 does not want to put data on
to the bus during a certain period of time. What should it
do? If it outputs logic 0 through its bus driver, then if
device 1 — which does want to put data on to the bus —
outputs logic 1, the two devices will be fighting for the
bus, one trying to pull it up to 1 while the other tries to
pull it down to 0. Similarly, if device 2 tries to detach
itself from the bus by driving it with logic 1, it will
interfere with device 1 if the latter tries to drive the bus
to logic 0.
TTL gates are not designed for this situation, and it is
not possible to forecast the result of such a fight by
considering the gates as logic elements. We must look at the
detailed circuitry of the output stage of a gate. This is
shown in Figure 2.6. (At this point you may need to refer
back to the entry on transistors in the glossary at the end

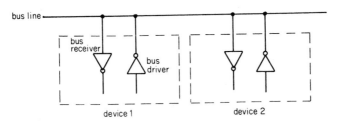

Figure 2.5 Two devices connected to a bus

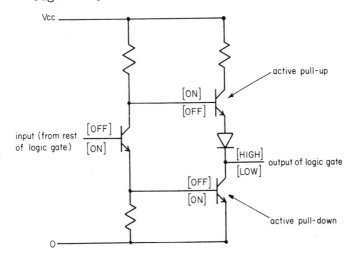

Figure 2.6 TTL "totem-pole" output stage

of the last chapter.) Two transistors are arranged in a
"totem-pole" configuration, one providing active pull-up
through the top transistor when the output is to be high, and
the other providing active pull-down through the bottom one
when it is to be low. This arrangement is used to increase
the switching speed of the device from one logic level to the
other, and to ensure that the drive capability of the device
is the same whether it is in a high or a low state. (The
"drive capability" is the number of other devices which can
be attached to its output without affecting the logic level.)
The figure is annotated to show the input and output levels
and the states of the transistors, when the output is high
(upper annotations) and low (lower annotations).

    Figure 2.7 sketches the totem-poles of two gates whose
outputs are connected together by a bus line, annotated with
the states that occur when device 1 is putting a high level
on to the bus and device 2 is driving it low. The result
will be that current flows as shown by the arrow — and it

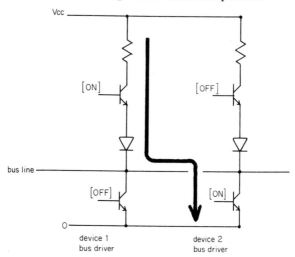

Figure 2.7 TTL "totem-poles" fighting for the bus

will be quite large. Its value can be calculated as Vcc
minus twice the collector-emitter drop minus one diode drop,
divided by the resistor value — about 30 mA with normal
component values. The bus line will probably end up at a low
logic level, but this will depend on how it is loaded by
other devices. Both output stages will get hot and may fail
— with 30 mA between a 5 volt Vcc and ground, 150 mW must be
dissipated. TTL is just not designed to operate in this way.

Open-Collector Gates

    One solution to the problem is to use "open-collector"
gates to drive the bus. These are TTL gates which do not
have active pull-up. Instead, the output is taken from the
collector of the pull-down transistor, which is otherwise
left open. Figure 2.8 shows the output stage of an open-
collector gate.
    Somewhere on the bus line, a bus termination resistor is
supplied to pull the line up to Vcc. Then, if any of the
open-collector gates which drive the bus has its output
transistor ON, this active pull-down will overcome the pull-
up resistor to bring the line to a low state. Only if all
the gates which drive the bus have their output transistor
OFF will the line float up to a high level. Thus a device
can logically detach itself from the bus by turning its
output transistor OFF, and then it will not interfere with a
device which wishes to drive the bus.

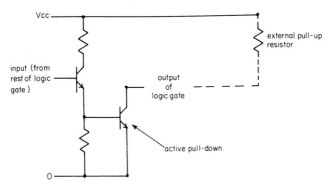

Figure 2.8 Open-collector output stage

You can see from the table in Figure 2.9 that if A is high, B's level is transferred faithfully to the bus, and vice versa. The table is in fact that of the logical AND function if the levels are interpreted in positive logic (LOW = logic 0, HIGH = logic 1), and the configuration is often called a "wired-AND" since the AND operation has been accomplished simply by a piece of wire. (You may come across the term "wired-OR": this — surprisingly — refers to exactly the same phenomenon, with a "negative logic" interpretation.)

There are two drawbacks to the use of open-collector gates to drive buses, both of which stem from the lack of active pull-up. Firstly, they are slow; and secondly, they are susceptible to noise. These can in fact be overcome if the termination is chosen carefully, taking into account the load on the bus line. However, the great attraction of a bus structure for interconnection of computer subsystems is the flexibility it offers for reconfiguration by inserting or removing modules, or extending the bus without adverse effect on the rest of the system — and this rules out the possibility of exactly matched termination.

Tri-State Gates

A simple alternative to open-collector driving, which has only appeared recently with the advent of CMOS (complementary metal-oxide semiconductor) logic, is the "tri-state gate". The CMOS logic family is often used for microprocessors, rather than TTL, and it turns out to be natural in CMOS to give gates a third, "disabled", state in which they do not affect the bus. The idea of a tri-state gate proved so useful that a TTL implementation was subsequently invented.

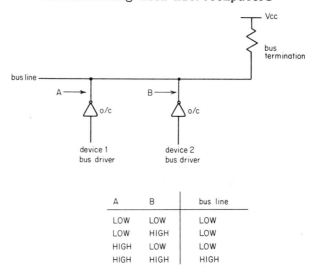

A	B	bus line
LOW	LOW	LOW
LOW	HIGH	LOW
HIGH	LOW	LOW
HIGH	HIGH	HIGH

Figure 2.9 Open-collector gates driving a bus

This retains the totem-pole output stage of ordinary TTL, but adds an extra "enable/disable" input to the gate which turns both the pull-up and the pull-down transistors off, overriding the logic input. The result is effectively to disconnect the gate from the bus if this input is asserted. Figure 2.10 shows the circuit. If the enable/disable input is high, the diodes prevent any current leakage through the enable/disable line and so the gate acts as normal. A low level on enable/disable, however, holds the base of the two transistors down and keeps them off. This automatically ensures that the third transistor is off also.

The symbol for several tri-state gates is shown in Figure 2.11. Buses are almost always driven by this type of gate nowadays, wherever possible. However, if the outputs of two tri-state gates are connected together via a bus line and both gates are enabled at the same time, the problem of excessive current consumption that we found with ordinary TTL gates reappears, and for some bus lines this rules out the possibility of tri-state driving. We will encounter examples of such lines later.

BUS SYNCHRONIZATION

Suppose device 1 wants to send data to device 2 along the bus of Figure 2.12. It puts the data on the data bus, and then puts the address of device 2 on the address bus. Device

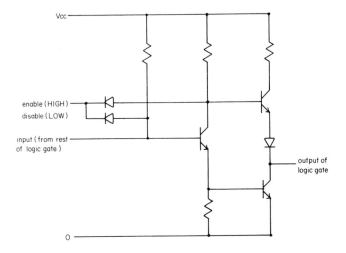

Figure 2.10 Tri-state output stage

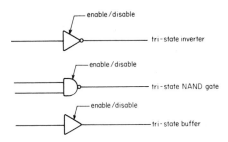

Figure 2.11 Logic symbols for tri-state gates

2 constantly monitors the address bus for its own address.
As soon as it sees it, it reads the data from the data bus.
Once the data has been read, device 1 can stop driving the
address and data buses, and do something else.   OK?
    No!   There are two problems with the above scenario.
Firstly, how does device 2 know when the address on the
address bus is valid?   Say the bus has just 3 lines (3-bit
addresses).   Then if it is initially at <100> and device 1
changes it to <010> to address device 2, there is a good
chance that it will transiently pass through <110> or <000>
during the change.   If all the devices on the bus continually
monitored the addresses, then the data would be incorrectly
sent to device <110> or <000> as well as to device <010>.
The second problem is, how does device 1 know when device 2

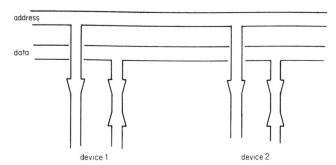

Figure 2.12 Two devices connected to a bus

has read the data bus?   Until it is sure, it must not remove
the data from the bus.

Synchronous Buses

   One solution to both these problems is to have a common
clock for all the devices. The clock produces the signal
shown in Figure 2.13.
   All devices obey the convention that

CONVENTION 1 — they only look at the bus when the clock is
               high.

Thus if device 1 changes the address lines, it must ensure
that it does so when the clock is low, and that the lines
have settled to their new levels by the next clock tick. The
clock line may as well be another bus line, as in Figure
2.14. This adds another group of lines to the bus, the
control lines, which so far contains just the clock. We will
see that more control lines are needed for asynchronous
buses, and to deal with bus contention.
   This solves the first problem. The address lines are only
valid at clock ticks, and when a bus device is addressed, it
recognizes its address at the next tick. It seems reasonable
to suppose that it will be able to read the data from the bus
at the same tick, leading to

CONVENTION 2 — a device takes one clock tick to read from
               the bus.

The sequence of events when device 1 sends data to device 2
is shown in Figure 2.15.
   A circuit to read from the bus will need an "address

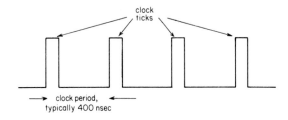

Figure 2.13 Clock signal for synchronous buses

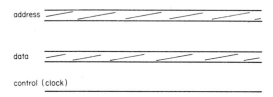

Figure 2.14 Synchronous bus

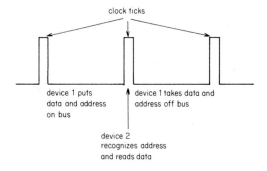

Figure 2.15 Transmission on a synchronous bus

decoder" to detect when the address lines are set to select
the device, and a register to receive the value that is read
from the data lines at the next clock tick. Such a circuit
is shown in Figure 2.16. There are three address lines, and
the address of the device is <010>. Eight data lines are
used, and the 8-bit register within the device holds the last
data word read.

   The bus structure that has been described is called a
"synchronous bus" because each device on it is driven from
the same clock. We have had to introduce two conventions,

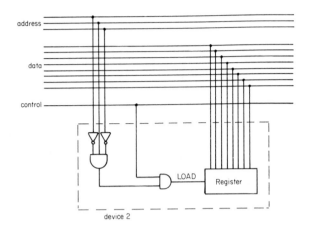

Figure 2.16 Reading from a synchronous bus

which together form the <u>bus</u> <u>protocol</u>. The bus will only work
as long as the protocol is observed correctly by all devices
attached to it. The idea of a protocol (dictionary
definition: "terms agreed upon as the basis of a formal
treaty") is an important one in all interactive communication
systems. What is the protocol for opening a telephone
conversation? — meeting your neighbour in the street? —
picking up a girl at a disco?
    The disadvantage of a synchronous bus is that all devices
on it must work at the same speed, because they are driven by
the same clock. Thus the bus must go at the speed of the
slowest device on it. For example, if we attach a store
module with access time 500 nsec (fast store) to the bus, and
another with an access time of 2 usec (slow store), we will
have to run the bus with a 2 usec clock and so do not gain
any advantage from having the fast store.

Asynchronous Buses

    Recall the two problems that were posed by bus
synchronization: the presence of spurious addresses during a
transition of the address lines, and the need to know when
data had been accepted by a device. The first problem can be
overcome by having an "address valid" control line which is
set to logic 1 by the sending device when it is sure that the
address lines have settled. The second needs a "data
accepted" line which is set to logic 1 by the receiving
device as soon as it has read the data (Figure 2.17).

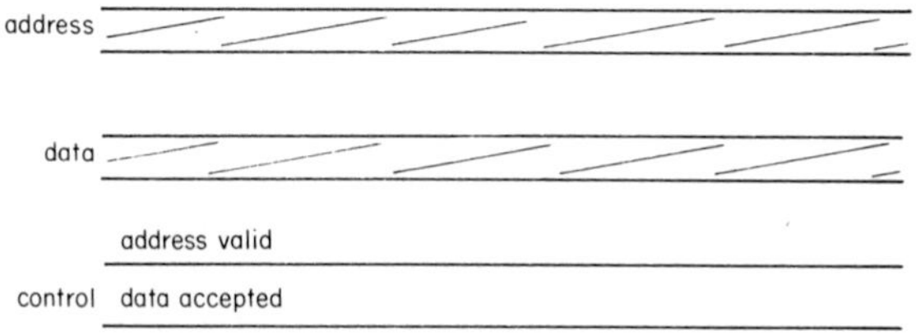

Figure 2.17 Asynchronous bus

This allows for devices of different speeds to operate
sensibly on the same bus. When the sending device has put
data and address on to the bus, and after it has waited for a
short time (typically 200 nsec) to ensure that the lines have
settled, it asserts "address valid". This is the signal for
all devices on the bus to examine the address lines to see if
the data is for them. If it is, they read the data
immediately, and then assert "data accepted". For a fast
device, this will take only a short time; whereas it will
take longer if the device is slow. In either case, as soon
as the sending device sees "data accepted" it can release the
bus lines and proceed to its next operation. Figure 2.18
shows the sequence of events.

This protocol is called "handshake" or "interlocked"
transmission. It uses a signal from the sender to assert
that the address and data lines have been set up, and a
response from the receiver to indicate that data has been
accepted. The result — transmission at the maximum speed
possible for the two devices. The price — two extra control
lines in the bus, and the risk of "hanging up" for ever if
things go wrong (imagine what could happen if the receiving
device did not work properly!).

In practice, the possibility of hanging up for ever can be
rather embarrassing. It only needs someone to run a program
which attempts to communicate with a non-existent device, or
to unplug a module from the bus, to bring the whole system to
a halt. Sometimes this is considered so dangerous that the
sender implements a time-out, where if the receiver has not
responded after a certain maximum time (say 10 usec) the
sender takes control again, probably to report a fault
condition. The time-out idea is important in all systems
which "fail soft", that is, do not collapse completely when
something goes wrong. People, of course, implement time-outs
automatically (what do you do when you answer a phone and
no-one speaks?).

The only difficulty with the protocol described is that
the time for which the receiver asserts "data accepted" has

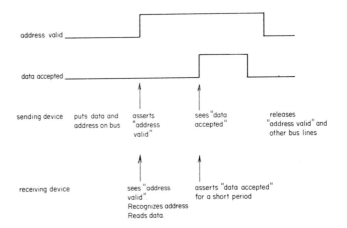

Figure 2.18 Transmission on an asynchronous bus

not been specified. If it asserts it for a very short time,
it may be missed by the sender. If it is asserted for too
long, the sender may be doing its next transmission and
falsely conclude that this too has been accepted. A solution
is for the receiver to assert "data accepted" until it sees
that "address valid" is no longer asserted. The sender
should then wait for the receiver to de-assert "data
accepted" before using the bus again. This protocol is
called "fully-interlocked" transmission (Figure 2.19).

Figure 2.20 shows a circuit to read from the bus using
fully-interlocked transmission. Note that the use of an
asynchronous bus does not necessarily imply that the devices
attached to it employ asynchronous logic: normally, as in
the figure, the devices have their own internal clocks. When
the receiver sees its address on the bus with "address valid"
asserted, it awaits the next clock pulse, and uses it to set
a flip-flop and load the bus data into the register. Since
this will happen (virtually) instantaneously, it
simultaneously gates "address valid" back on to the "data
accepted" bus line. If the load operation were to take
longer, the device could be designed to wait until its
completion before asserting "data accepted" to prevent the
sender from altering the state of the bus. Note the use of a
tri-state gate to drive the bus: the driver is enabled
whenever the address lines are recognized. (This may result
in driving the bus line during address transients, but no
harm will come because the sender will not be looking at
"data accepted" during transients.)

While the device is addressed and "address valid" is high,

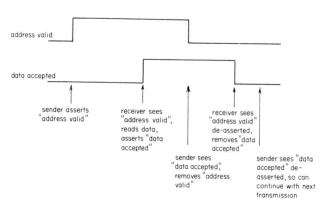

Figure 2.19 Fully-interlocked transmission

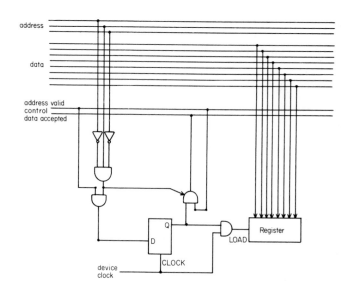

Figure 2.20 Reading from a fully-interlocked bus

successive ticks of the device clock will repeatedly load the
register with the contents of the data bus. Only on the tick
after "address valid" is de-asserted does the output of the
flip-flop go low, ceasing to load the register. Hence the
master is obliged to hold the data on the bus until it sees
"data accepted" asserted — and this is part of the bus
protocol.

READ AND WRITE CONTROL

So far, we have assumed in our examples that device 1 was
sending data to device 2. Suppose that device 2 is the
processor and device 1 a store. Since the store will usually
hold more than one word of data, it will respond to several
different combinations of the address lines, each of which
combinations addresses a certain location of the store.
Typically, there will be 16 address lines, and a single store
unit may have 2^{12} locations, each holding one byte of data.
So 12 of the 16 lines are used to select the location within
the store, and the other 4 address the storage device itself.
Thus, device 2 will respond to all the addresses in the
range, say, <0110000000000000> to <0110111111111111>. This
presents no problems with address decoding.

We have discussed the case where device 1 — the processor
— is writing data to device 2 — the store. The processor
also needs to be able to read from the store. In this case
it is still the initiator of the data transfer, but the
transfer is in the other direction — from the store to the
processor.

There are two relationships here: the master/slave
relation between devices 1 and 2, and the
receiver/transmitter relation. Device 1 is the master in all
the cases we have considered, since it initiates the bus
activity; and device 2 is the slave. In the case of a write
from device 1 to device 2, the former is the transmitter and
the latter the receiver, whereas for a read from device 2 to
device 1 these roles are reversed — without affecting the
master/slave relationship.

The choice between reading and writing is accomplished
simply by adding a "read/write" control line to the bus,
which is held low by device 1 for a read and high for a write
(Figure 2.21).

If only one device can ever initiate transfers along the
bus — in the sense that a processor can initiate a read or a

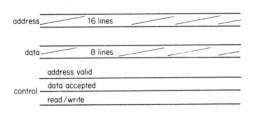

Figure 2.21 Asynchronous bus, without contention

write from a store, but a store cannot itself initiate these operations — we now have all the control lines that are needed. However, if there are several devices that can initiate bus activity, for example, several processors, we encounter some interesting problems.

BUS CONTENTION

At any time, at most one device must be capable of initiating transfers on the bus. This device is called the "bus master". If several devices are potential bus masters (imagine several processors on the same bus), there must be some protocol for passing mastership from one to the other as needed.

What kind of a system could have several potential bus masters? Glance back at Figure 2.1. In the absence of the dashed line, the processor is the only potential bus master. The dashed line introduces the possibility of a transfer being initiated by an input/output interface, and the interface in question will therefore be a potential bus master. Table 2.1 summarizes which devices are potential masters.

The ideal bus structure is one where every potential master uses the same protocol to communicate with other devices, and none is in overall charge. This increases the reliability of the system, since any device can fail without disrupting bus activity that does not involve it. If, on the other hand, just one of the devices had responsibility for the organization of the bus, its failure could be catastrophic. We will stray from this ideal in the following two sections in order to see how existing computer systems operate their buses, but return to it later to examine more

	potential bus master
processor	yes
store	no
i/o interface ⟨ slow device (e.g. teletype)	no
i/o interface ⟨ fast device (e.g. disk)	yes

Table 2.1 Potential bus masters

unconventional "distributed" bus protocols.

The Bus Controller

"Bus contention" occurs when two devices both desire bus
mastership. The best cure for contention is prevention! A
"bus busy" control line is added to show when the bus is
active. This is asserted by the bus master throughout its
mastership. There is normally no mechanism to prevent a
device from hogging the bus for ever: it is assumed that
device designers understand the importance of leaving the bus
free whenever possible.
A device requests mastership only when the bus is not
busy. Suppose it does so by asserting "bus busy". This by
itself may seem an adequate protocol for transferring
mastership. Unfortunately it is not. If two devices
simultaneously assert "bus busy", they will each think they
have the bus to themselves, resulting in collisions. Hence
there must be a protocol for requesting bus mastership, and
having it granted by a central authority — the bus
controller. A "bus request" and a "bus grant" line are
introduced for this purpose. The controller monitors "bus
busy" and "bus request", and issues grants when appropriate.
Figure 2.22 shows the control lines so far.
However, the "bus grant" line as described does not
completely solve the problem. Each device requesting the bus
will see the grant line being asserted, and each will think
that it is now bus master. One way out is to "daisy-chain"
the "bus grant" line through the devices, as in Figure 2.23.
A device, seeing "bus grant", will only pass the signal on to
the next device if it does not want the bus itself. Hence a
device has priority over all other devices which are further
away from the controller than it, when contention occurs.
Figure 2.23 also shows the circuitry which controls the
daisy-chaining. When a device wants mastership, it takes the
"bus requested" signal high. This signals a request on the

| address valid |
| data accepted |
| read/write |
| bus busy |
| bus request |
| bus grant |

Figure 2.22 Bus control lines

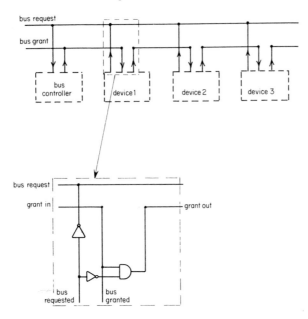

Figure 2.23 Daisy-chaining of the "bus grant" line

"bus request" line. Note that this line <u>cannot</u> be tri-state, since there is no way of preventing simultaneous bus requests, and more than one tri-state gate must not actively drive the same line at the same time. It is the only bus line we have introduced that must be wired-AND, and an open-collector gate is shown driving it low to signal a request. If the "grant in" line is asserted, it is routed through to the "grant out" line provided the bus has not been requested. If it has, the grant chain is broken and the device achieves mastership.

A summary of the protocol necessary for a device to gain and relinquish bus mastership is given in Figure 2.24. The bus is used for a single "write" operation during mastership. Although the protocol is quite complicated, we have seen how each step is necessary if the bus is to perform its job correctly.

Bus Arbitration

An alternative to daisy-chaining the "bus grant" signal is to have separate "bus request" and "bus grant" lines for each device, as shown in Figure 2.25. When contention occurs, the bus controller can select one of the contending devices and

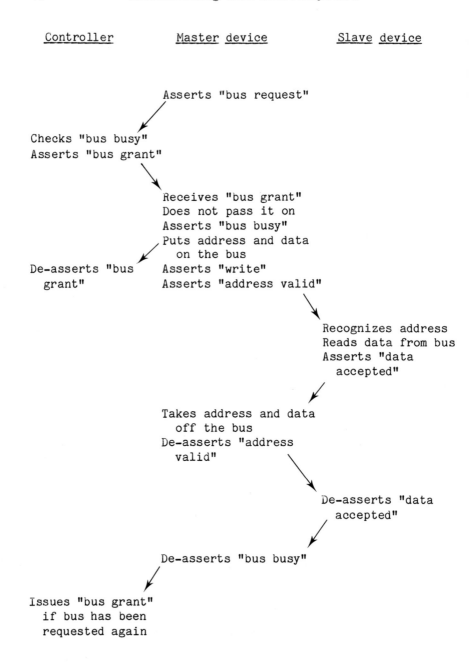

<u>Controller</u>   <u>Master</u> <u>device</u   <u>Slave</u> <u>device</u>

Asserts "bus request"

Checks "bus busy"
Asserts "bus grant"

Receives "bus grant"
Does not pass it on
Asserts "bus busy"
Puts address and data
    on the bus
De-asserts "bus   Asserts "write"
    grant"   Asserts "address valid"

Recognizes address
Reads data from bus
Asserts "data
    accepted"

Takes address and data
    off the bus
De-asserts "address
    valid"

De-asserts "data
    accepted"

De-asserts "bus busy"

Issues "bus grant"
    if bus has been
    requested again

Figure 2.24 Protocol for gaining bus mastership and sending
            data

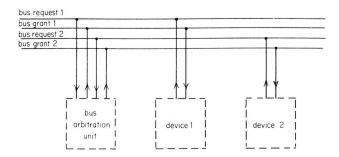

Figure 2.25 Bus control with an arbitration unit

give it alone mastership by asserting its grant line. In this case, the controller is in a position to impose a priority structure on devices using programmed priority levels, and is often called a "bus arbitration unit".

The disadvantage of bus arbitration is that the number of lines increases by two for each device added. However, the delays inevitably associated with a long daisy-chain are avoided. In practice a compromise solution is sometimes adopted, with say 8 priority levels, 8 "bus request" and "bus grant" lines, and several devices daisy-chained within each priority level.

Distributed Buses

Is it possible to have a bus structure where each device connected to it communicates using the same protocol, and there is no central bus controller or arbitration unit? In general, if several identical autonomous devices are connected to a single bus, there is no way of guaranteeing that two or more of them do not try to use it at the same time. However, if such "collisions" can be detected, it is possible to devise protocols for re-transmission which ensure that the information gets through eventually.

Although it should be possible to detect collisions by looking for the neither-high-nor-low logic level that occurs when two tri-state gates, both enabled, are fighting for the bus, in practice distributed buses usually use <u>serial transmission</u>. So far, we have viewed the bus as a parallel collection of wires, where the address, data and control information is presented in parallel, one wire for each bit of the information. However, if bus wires are expensive, it is more attractive to use one line only for the information, and transmit the bits one after another on this one wire.

This is the case, for example, when radio is used as the bus medium: to transmit 32 bits in parallel requires 32 different radio frequencies to be reserved for the bus, and radio bandwidth is a scarce resource. (The cost of duplicating the radio receiver and transmitter 32 times for each device connected to the bus is not negligible either!)

To detect collisions using serial transmission, some error-checking information is sent with the data. For example, one might send each transmission twice, and the receiver could check that they were the same. It is extremely unlikely that in the event of a collision when two transmitters are driving the bus simultaneously, the duplicate versions will check correctly. In fact, there are much more economical collision-detection mechanisms than double transmission, but we need not be concerned with them here — the principle is enough.

When a receiver sees a transmission addressed to it, it sends a "data accepted" or "acknowledgement" message. If, on the other hand, a collision has occurred and the transmission is corrupted, it remains silent. If the sender has not received acknowledgement of his transmission after a reasonable time, he should assume that it has collided, and re-transmit it. However, if two senders collide on a transmission, it is important that they should not time out after exactly the same interval and collide when sending again, and so on ad infinitum! This situation is avoided by the simple expedient of making the time-out interval random (within suitable bounds).

What if an acknowledgement is corrupted by colliding with someone else's transmission? It will simply fail to be received. The device which was expecting the acknowledgement will then time out and transmit again. This means that the receiver will see the same message twice, and care should be taken to ensure that this does not have any harmful effects. For example, each message could be numbered, so that the receiver can simply throw away the second message after acknowledging it.

The scheme described is used in the Aloha network of computers in the Hawaiian islands. Note that no attempt is made to detect if the bus is busy before sending: this means that collisions can be expected fairly often and much of the bus's capacity will be used for re-transmissions. (One way of calculating just how much — under very simple assumptions — is given as an Appendix.) A more sophisticated mechanism is for the sender to listen to the bus before transmitting, to see if it will cause a collision by interfering with another transmission. This is analogous to the "bus busy" information described earlier. While this can be expected to reduce substantially the frequency of collisions, it will not eliminate them altogether since two devices may still decide to send at exactly the same time. A further refinement is for the sender to monitor its transmission itself and check that the bits it "hears" are the same as those it sends. If there is a discrepancy, this indicates a collision and the sender should cease transmitting at once. However, this refinement is not feasible in the case of radio, since locally transmitted signals tend to swamp the local receiver and so collisions are not detected locally.

SUMMARY

Subsystems of a computer are usually connected together by a common bus, instead of by connecting each subsystem to every other one individually. A bus is a passive device — just a bundle of wires. However, to make it work, a logical superstructure of protocol and convention must be adopted, and observed correctly by every device connected to the bus. If any one device fails to observe the protocol, it can disrupt all communications along the bus. This is the price of a common bus.

The bus wires are divided into three groups: address, data, and control. Address lines select the particular device for which the current communication (be it read or write) is intended. The data lines transmit the data. The control lines are not a homogeneous group — each is for a different purpose. Buses having different protocols will have different uses for the control lines.

Because a bus is bi-directional, it cannot be driven with ordinary TTL gates. Tri-state gates are particularly suitable when it is known in advance which device is going to drive the bus lines over a particular period of time. This is true for the address and data lines, and most of the control lines. However, some control lines — notably "bus request" — may be driven simultaneously by two or more devices. For these, tri-state gates are not adequate and the lines must be driven by open-collector gates.

Bus devices can be synchronized together by making one of the control lines a clock. However, this has the effect of forcing all transfers on the bus to proceed at the rate of the slowest device — even when the two devices which take part in the transfer are much faster. Hence asynchronous buses are usually employed, where a "data accepted" line is driven by the receiving device to indicate that it has read

the data on the bus.
    Bus contentions are difficult to resolve. One solution is
to have a "bus controller" or "bus arbitration unit" which
has sole responsibility for deciding which device is to have
the bus when contention occurs. This usually means that the
"bus grant" signal generated by the controller must be
daisy-chained between the various devices, and not bused
straight across. It is possible to implement distributed
buses which do not have an arbitration unit in overall
charge. The price that must be paid is a certain amount of
re-transmission when collisions occur. The number of re-
transmissions can be reduced but not eliminated by suitably
sophisticated protocols.

FURTHER READING

Abramson, N. (1970) The ALOHA system — another alternative
    for computer communications, AFIPS Conference Proceedings
    37, 281-285.
    I don't know of any book that treats distributed
    buses — you have to go back to the original
    research papers. This one describes the Aloha
    system that was mentioned above.

Davies, D.W. and Barber, D.L.A. (1973) "Communication
    Networks for Computers." Wiley, London.
    The protocols we have seen are very simple in
    comparison with those that are needed for data
    transfers between computers. Chapter 11 of this
    authoritative book on computer networks shows
    just how complicated protocols can become for
    transferring data reliably between remote
    computers.

Metcalfe, R.M. and Boggs, D.R. (1976) Ethernet: distributed
    packet switching for local computer networks,
    Communications of the ACM 19, 395-404.
    This paper describes how the Aloha system can be
    improved by the sender monitoring the bus and
    only transmitting if there is no other traffic on
    it.

Peatman, J.B. (1977) "Microcomputer-based Design." McGraw
    Hill, New York.
    This is an excellent book on most aspects of
    microcomputer hardware and interfacing. It

contains quite a lot of information on the bus,
describing in detail how to connect devices to it
(Chapter 3).

Williams, G.E. (1977) "Digital Technology: Principles and
  Practices." Science Research Associates, Chicago.
  Describes the circuitry of TTL, open-collector,
  and tri-state gates in some detail (Chapter 2).
  Also includes a brief section on buses (Chapter
  12).

APPENDIX: TRAFFIC ON A DISTRIBUTED BUS

   Suppose d devices are attached to a distributed bus, each
of which sends m messages (excluding re-transmissions) per
second. All messages take T seconds to transmit. A
synchronous or interlocked bus could handle the traffic
provided the total time for dm messages was less than 1
second, i.e. provided

   $dmT < 1.$

   Now let the rate of re-transmissions be r per second. In
100 seconds, there will be 100d(m+r) messages sent (including
re-transmissions). These will occupy a total of 100d(m+r)T
seconds, which must of course be less than 100, and during
the remaining 100 - 100d(m+r)T seconds the bus will be
unused. Hence the probability of a message requiring re-
transmission is 100d(m+r)T/100. Now since there are r re-
transmissions for m real messages, the re-transmission rate
can also be expressed as r/m. Hence

   $r/m = 100d(m + r)T/100,$

from which

$$r = \frac{dm^2T}{1 - dmT}.$$

We observed above that 100d(m+r)T must be less than 100
seconds, since the bus cannot be used more than full-time.
Hence

$$d \left(m + \frac{dm^2T}{1 - dmT} \right) T < 1,$$

or $\quad \dfrac{dmT}{1 - dmT} < 1,$

or   dmT < 1/2.

This shows that the maximum number of messages that can be
originated under the distributed bus organization is only
half that which the bus could handle if control were
centralized.
    Actually, these calculations are rather simplified. In
real life, even a bus with centralized control cannot
necessarily handle the traffic if dmT is close to 1, because
this is the average load — the peak load will be higher. If
messages are generated stochastically, then the performance
of a centralized bus will depend on whether messages can be
queued by the devices that originate them. For example,
suppose a device wants to send a message, but the
(centralized) bus is busy. It must wait for the bus to
become free. What if, while it is waiting, another message
appears which must be sent as well? The device needs to be
able to queue the two messages. If it can't, then a message
will be lost and so the bus must be overloaded. If it can,
how many messages can be queued? Two? Two hundred? This is
one of the parameters that will affect the performance of a
bus with centralized control. In the most optimistic case,
where an unlimited number of messages can be queued by each
device if necessary, the centralized bus will be able to
operate provided dmT < 1. Statistical calculations show that
the Aloha distributed bus becomes saturated if dmT grows as
big as 1/2e. Thus the distributed bus can handle about 20%
of the traffic that a centralized bus can.

Microcomputer Interfaces

Consider how the same information can be represented in different ways, like marks on paper, or speech sounds. An interface is a connection between one information representation and another. Computer interfaces convert between the computer's representation, namely electrical signals on the bus, and another representation — like dots of light on a display screen, or a musical note. There is an obvious distinction between input and output interfaces. (What is not obvious is which is which: it is conventional to look at things from the computer's point of view, so that "input" means from the outside world to the computer.)

Interfaces provide a means of communication between the outside world and the computer. Contrast this with the buses that we studied in the last chapter, which provide communication within the computer system itself. Communication along a bus is entirely in the form of binary electrical signals. The information to be transmitted falls naturally into logically separate groups: address, data, and control. The control part is the most interesting, and depends on the protocol which is adopted for information transfer. Each control line has a different purpose, and each is necessary if the protocol is to be observed. All in all, the subject of buses is well-defined and satisfyingly logical.

Interfaces are a different matter. They take us closer to the real world, with all its variety and hazards. For a start, there is a multitude of different representations of information. To interface to a car engine, the throttle position, mixture control, engine speed and temperature, and ignition timing all need to be converted or controlled.

Where does interfacing end and mechanical engineering begin?
To interface to smells, we need to study chemistry. What
about transmission of information between the computer and a
remote device which converts it to another representation —
is this part of the interface? There is no clean logical
structure to the subject of interfacing; no neat division
between the interface and the real world. Nevertheless,
interfaces must be understood, designed, and built, and this
is probably the most important single area in the application
of microprocessors to man-machine communication. For
example, lack of a cheap car engine interface and smell
interface is the chief reason why automatic anti-pollution
controls for vehicle engines — which would benefit everyone
by improving petrol consumption and reducing pollution — are
not commonly used.

The subject of interfaces could go on for ever. This
chapter covers its most important aspects, with particular
regard to microcomputer interfaces. We begin by looking at
some simple input and output peripherals, including the
principles of converting between digital and analogue
electrical representations, and the use of optical
transducers to detect the position of objects. Interfacing
to the bus is simplified by LSI (large-scale integration)
integrated circuit chips, some of which are described. If
the peripheral device is remote from the processor, serial
transmission is often used, where only one wire carries a
word of data and the bits follow each other along it. This
eliminates both the need for expensive multi-core cables, and
the hazard of "cross-talk" between wires running in parallel
(where the data on one wire can, by electrical propagation,
degrade that on its neighbours). The principle of
asynchronous serial transmission is covered, as is the
problem of converting between the parallel and serial
representations. Again, LSI chips are available to perform
this conversion.

Thus far, we have said very little about the role of the
bus in interfacing. The reason for this is simply that
connecting to the bus is easy: the tricky part of the
interface is that which connects with the outside world, be
it the world of light, analogue electronics, serial data
transmission, or whatever. However, the synchronization of
external devices with the processor must be considered, and
two important techniques for this are outlined next.
Finally, the process of DMA (direct memory access) transfer
is described, where the peripheral can become bus master and
transmit information along the bus independently of the
processor.

LIGHTS AND SWITCHES

The simplest output peripheral is a bank of on/off LEDs
(light-emitting diodes), which emit light when they conduct
current. If eight LEDs are provided, then one data word can
be displayed. To keep the LEDs alight, the data from the bus
can either be latched into flip-flops, or periodically re-
generated ("refreshed") by the processor. If LEDs are
refreshed 20 or more times a second for a millisecond or more
each, an illusion of continuous illumination is achieved.

The input device corresponding to a bank of LEDs is a row
of switches. Switches themselves are bi-stable devices, so
latching is unnecessary. There is, however, a serious
problem with contact bouncing. Figure 3.2 shows a typical

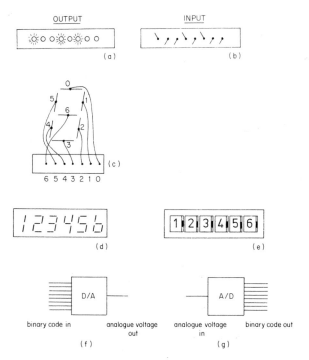

Figure 3.1 Simple input and output peripherals
    (a) Bank of LEDs
    (b) Bank of switches
    (c) 7-segment display
    (d) Bank of 7-segment displays
    (e) Bank of thumbwheels
    (f) D/A converter
    (g) A/D converter

waveform generated when a switch is changed from open to
closed. The output does not change cleanly, as you might
expect, but passes through a transition phase where it
oscillates randomly. Unless appropriate precautions are
taken, this will cause chaos if interfaced directly to a
microprocessor. As with display refresh, the precautions can
be taken in either hardware or software.

A hardware debouncing circuit is also shown in Figure 3.2.
It relies on a break-before-make switch action, so that no
matter how unclean the switch output is as one contact is
broken and as the other is made, the "breaking" is completely
finished before the "making" begins. Then, the first "make"
spike which exceeds the threshold for logic 1 will activate
the latch, and it will remain in the new state throughout the
rest of the "making" disturbance. Software debouncing uses a
different principle. The program waits for a specified time
(usually around 20 msec) after a change in switch value is
detected, before reading the switch and returning the new
value.

A 7-segment display contains seven LED segments arranged

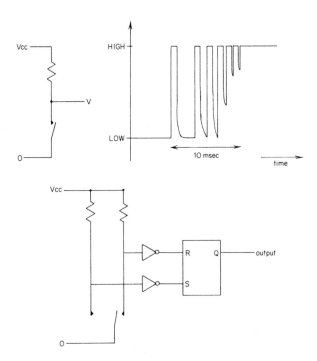

Figure 3.2 Switching waveform, and a debouncing circuit

so that the numerals can be shown. The lights are connected
to bits in the data word as shown in Figure 3.1(c). Binary
patterns for the digits are

0	<00111111>	5	<01101111>
1	<00000110>	6	<01111100>
2	<01011011>	7	<00000111>
3	<01001111>	8	<01111111>
4	<01100110>	9	<01100111>.

Again, the data may either be latched, or refreshed by the
processor. The problems of latching are highlighted when
several banks of 7-segment displays are used. If there are
six displays in a bank, 6 x 7 = 42 latches must be supplied
for each. With several banks, a fair-sized store is needed
to hold the latched bits. But the microcomputer already has
a store! — accessible to the processor. Use can be made of
this providing the processor is prepared to undertake to
refresh the segments regularly. The input device
corresponding to a 7-segment display is a thumbwheel.

If enough LED segments are incorporated in the display,
alphabetic characters can be presented as well as digits.
Figure 3.3 shows a 16-segment "starburst" display, together
with some examples of upper-case letters. Sixteen bits are
needed to define a character. In fact it is simpler and
often cheaper to provide a local store with the display
hardware instead of sharing the microcomputer's main store
and demanding regular refresh by the processor. You can buy
banks of 16-segment displays, complete with refresh
circuitry, which connect to the bus and appear as ordinary
memory locations to the processor — except that whenever it
writes to them the pattern on the appropriate display is
changed. We will return to this technique of making a
display appear as ordinary store in Chapter 4.

Another kind of inexpensive LED output device is a bar

Figure 3.3 Starburst display

display, which can be used to show the magnitude of a
changing quantity in an easily-perceived way. A handful of
LED's are placed side by side, and the quantity is indicated
in thermometer fashion by illuminating an appropriate number
of them. Figure 3.4 shows a simple circuit to drive such a
bar display with 8 LED's (in practice, many more than this
are usually employed). A 3-bit input is decoded into 8
lines, one and only one of which goes high for a given input
code. If these 8 lines were connected directly to the LED's,
only one would light up at a time, so a chain of OR-gates is
used to activate all of the LED's below the one which is
selected, as well. This provides a thermometer-style display
which can replace an ordinary electro-mechanical meter.

To input alphanumeric information we need to combine an
array of switches into a keyboard. Although a series of
individual switches like that of Figure 3.2 could be used,
this produces a rather inefficient coding, needing 16 bits
for 16 switches. Since the number of connections is a
dominant cost in microcomputer systems, more economical
coding techniques are used for keyboards where it is known
that only one key should be depressed at a time.

Figure 3.5 shows the circuit of a 16-key matrix assembly.
To drive it, the voltages on lines A-D are controlled and
those on lines E-H are read. If A is forced low and B-D are
all high, and at most one key is depressed, then the state of
switches 1-4 can be read on lines E-H. By altering the
voltages on A-D the positions of the other 12 switches can be
ascertained, a row at a time:

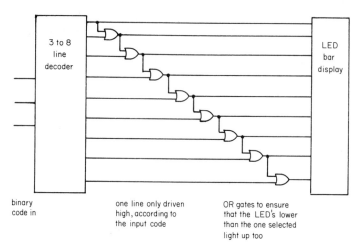

binary   one line only driven   OR gates to ensure
code in   high, according to   that the LED's lower
                      the input code   than the one selected
                                                  light up too

Figure 3.4 Circuit to drive a bar display

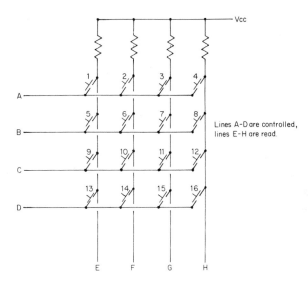

Figure 3.5 A keyboard matrix

voltage placed on A,B,C,D   keys read by examining E,F,G,H

low	high	high	high	1	2	3	4
high	low	high	high	5	6	7	8
high	high	low	high	9	10	11	12
high	high	high	low	13	14	15	15

If two or more keys in different columns are depressed
simultaneously, it will be possible to deduce which they are.
However, if two keys in the same column are depressed, say 1
and 5, a low voltage on A and a high one on B will fight, and
to avoid damage open-collector driving should be used.

The four lines A-D can be driven from two bits emanating
from the processor by a 2-to-4 line decoder. However, if the
lines E-H are encoded into two bits for input there will be
problems if more than one key is accidentally pressed at
once. (Can you see why?) Hence two output bits and four
input bits are usually used to drive such a keyboard matrix.
Of course, key debouncing is still necessary: this can be
done by hardware or software.

CONVERSION BETWEEN ANALOGUE AND DIGITAL

Computer systems often need to communicate with devices
with analogue electrical inputs and outputs. A D/A converter

(digital-to-analogue) takes a binary signal and produces an output voltage whose size is determined by the input. Usually the relationship between output and input is linear, although non-linear (e.g. logarithmic) D/A's do exist. Suppose the output range is 0-10 V, and the input is 8 bits. Then an input of <00000001> will give 1 x 10/256 = 0.04 V output, <10000000> will give 128 x 10/256 = 5 V output, and so on. The use of an 8-bit input implies a precision of 1/256 = 0.4%. If more accuracy is required by the analogue signal, then more input bits must be used — 10 bits, 12 bits, or even 14 bits. (Actually, it is hard to imagine the analogue side of a D/A converter justifying the precision implied by 14-bit conversion — $1/2^{14}$ = 0.006%!) An A/D converter (analogue-to-digital) performs the opposite conversion, taking as input an analogue voltage (say between 0 and 10 V) and producing the corresponding binary value as output.

Figure 3.6 shows the circuit of a simple D/A. It works by converting each "1" bit in the input to a current with a weighting appropriate to the position of that bit in the word, summing the currents, and converting the result back into a voltage. B0 to B7 are switches driven by the 8 bits of the input. When closed, they route the constant voltage E (say 10 V) through a weighting resistor into an amplifier. The resistors are chosen to give each bit an appropriately large or small influence on the overall output. The operational amplifier sums the currents produced in the resistors, with the R/2 feedback resistor ensuring that the most significant bit (B7) accounts for exactly half of the total analogue output range.

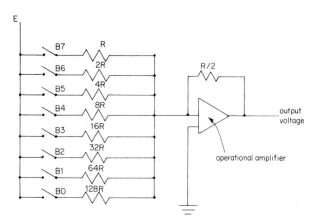

Figure 3.6 8-bit unsigned D/A converter

There are problems with the D/A of Figure 3.6. Resistors
don't come in binary-related values. Furthermore, if the
overall accuracy is to be 0.4%, in accordance with the 8-bit
input used, then the largest resistor must have 0.4%
tolerance — a stringent requirement. These difficulties can
be circumvented by more sophisticated D/A circuits, which
employ a network of equal resistors, called a "ladder
network", cunningly connected together to achieve the effect
of binary-related values. Ladder networks can be bought as
single integrated circuits, thus ensuring that variations of
resistance with temperature apply almost equally to all
resistors in the network and hence do not affect the overall
performance of the circuit. However, Figure 3.6 shows the
basic principle of conversion.

The most common types of A/D converter are made from a D/A
converter and a voltage comparator. Figure 3.7 shows one
possibility. An 8-bit counter counts up from zero. Its
output is D/A converted continuously and compared with the
input voltage. While it is smaller, the counter keeps
counting. As soon as it exceeds the input voltage, counting
is stopped and the "ready" line is activated to indicate that
the conversion is finished.

Again, there are problems with the circuit. The
inevitable transients during counting will produce terrible
spikes on the D/A output. The most fundamental problem,
however, is that the conversion takes a long time, especially
if the input voltage is near the top of its range. Again,
these difficulties can be overcome. For example, the counter
can be started at its previous final value and counted up or
down depending on the sign of the comparison. This will

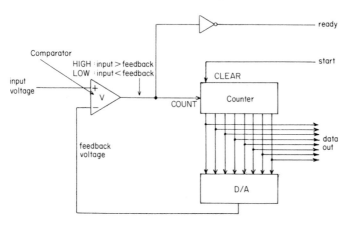

Figure 3.7 Making an A/D converter from a D/A converter

greatly speed up conversion if the input voltage does not
exhibit large discontinuities. However, Figure 3.7
illustrates the principle of A/D conversion.

OPTICAL INTERFACES

   Although many techniques for measuring real-world
variables involve translating information into analogue
electrical form and subsequent A/D conversion, there are a
number of things which can be measured directly in digital
form. Such measurements often use photodiodes, which detect
the presence of light and produce a logic 1 or 0 voltage
accordingly. For example, this provides a natural way of
counting objects on a conveyer belt, by arranging that they
occlude a beam of light as they proceed past a measuring
point.
   Figure 3.8 shows the paper-feed mechanism of a printing
press. A blank sheet of paper is picked up (using a vacuum
technique) by a "flight bar", which drags it along the
paper-table into the printing mechanism where it is printed
and ejected on to a stack of printed sheets. Then the flight
bar returns underneath the paper-table to pick up another
sheet. The number of sheets processed can be counted by a
photodiode shown at position B.
   Often, a straightforward count is not enough, and some
simple logic must be used prior to counting. For example, in
Figure 3.8 each flight bar continues to circulate regularly,
even though — for various reasons — it may fail to pick up
a blank sheet, in which case the press fails to produce a
page. Thus some of the flight bars' journeys are wasted. To
detect the actual number of pages printed a second photodiode
is placed at A to show the flight-bar traversals. The output
of the two photodiodes can be communicated via the bus to the
processor, and a program implements the logic necessary to
produce a count of actual pages.
   Another kind of optical measurement detects angular
position. A wheel is marked with reflecting and non-
reflecting paint as shown in Figure 3.9, and three
photodiodes detect light reflected by the wheel to ascertain
which of 8 angular positions it is in. For the binary coding
of Figure 3.9(a), imperfections in the painting will cause
spurious codes to be read as the wheel passes from one of the
8 positions to another. To avoid this, a "Gray code", shown
in Figure 3.9(b), is often used, where only one bit changes
at a time. Compare a 3-bit binary code with a Gray code,

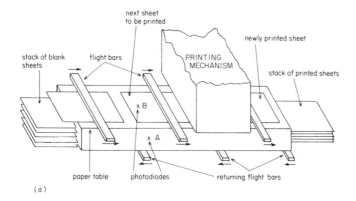

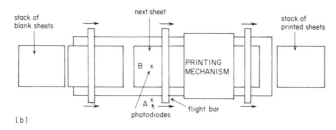

Figure 3.8 Paper-feed mechanism of a printing press
(a) Perspective
(b) Top view

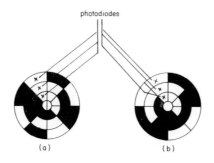

Figure 3.9 Optical detection of angular position
(a) Binary code
(b) Gray code

decimal: 0   1   2   3   4   5   6   7   (0)
binary: 000 001 010 011 100 101 110 111 (000)
Gray: 000 001 011 010 110 111 101 100 (000)

and notice how in the passage from 3 to 4, for example, all
three bits of the binary code change while only one of the
Gray code does.

A very common use of an optical interface, surprisingly
enough, is to transform binary electrical information into
binary electrical information! When two electronic devices
are connected together, it is often necessary to isolate one
from the other electrically because of the damaging effects
that transient currents in one might have on the other.
Optical isolation, where the sending device drives a LED and
the receiver used a photodiode to detect whether light is
present or not, provides a convenient, fast, and reliable
method of connection.

INTERFACE DEVICES

Figure 3.10 shows a D/A converter connected to a bus via
an interface device. But wait! The bus is parallel. The
D/A converter needs a parallel input. Why not connect it
directly to the bus and dispense with the interface device?

Why not? Consider the operations that must be performed.
They are:

    address decoding
    handling of read/write, address valid, data accepted, and

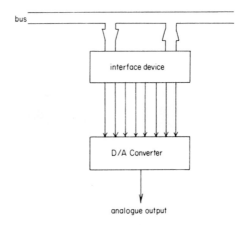

Figure 3.10 Interfacing a D/A converter to the bus

        reset lines
    data latching
    electrical buffering
    interrupt logic.

We met the first two operations in the last chapter. (The
"reset" control line is asserted at power-up, to initialize
all devices attached to the bus.) Data latching is needed
because the data is only present on the bus for a short time.
Electrical buffering is often necessary when reading from a
bus because many devices may be attached to it and
precautions must be taken not to overload the lines
electrically. Interrupt logic, which is essentially a way of
signalling to the processor that new data is ready (for
input) or needed (for output), will be described later.
    An output interface that performs most of the tasks is
shown in Figure 3.11. The data register assembly forms the
basis of an interface device which goes under various names
used by different manufacturers, such as "parallel output
port", "PIA", (programmable interface adapter), "VIA"
(versatile interface adapter), "PIO", (parallel input/output
interface), "MILE" (microprocessor interface latch element).
The address decoding function is not normally a part of the
interface device, because with a 16-bit address bus 32 extra
pins would have to be provided on the integrated circuit —
16 for the address bus and 16 for the desired interface
address — and circuits with lots of pins are difficult to
manufacture and use.

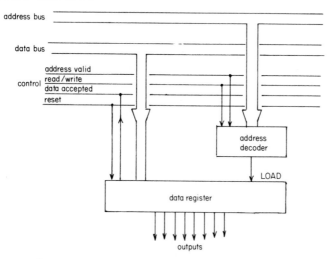

Figure 3.11 A simple output port

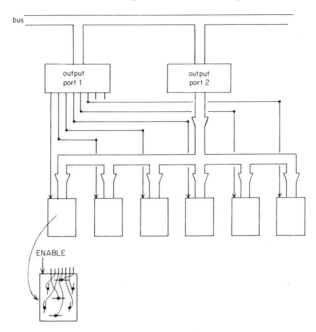

Figure 3.12 Interfacing a bank of 7-segment displays to a bus

Example

    To drive a bank of six 7-segment displays, six separate
parallel output ports could be used. However, they cost
money (5 to 10 pounds each). A more elegant solution, which
uses only 2 output ports, is shown in Figure 3.12. In this
circuit, port 1 selects one of the six displays to be
refreshed, while port 2 gives the data for the segments of
that display.
    The output transfers that must be accomplished by the
processor for one refresh cycle are shown in Figure 3.13.
One of the 6 binary patterns <10000000>, <01000000>,
<00100000>, <00010000>, <00001000>, or <00000100>, is written
to port 1 to select just one of the displays, and the
7-segment code for that display is written to port 2. Care
is taken to write zero to port 2 before changing the address,
to prevent the transient appearance of the wrong pattern on
the newly-selected display.
    The simple output port of Figure 3.11 is sometimes
combined, on the same chip, with an input port. A more
versatile interface allows each of the lines from the port to
be programmed as an input or an output. A <u>data direction</u>
<u>register</u> within the interface is used to indicate which are

```
<01101111>        ->        output port 2 (code for "5")
<10000000>        ->        output port 1
                  wait 1 msec
<00000000>        ->        output port 1
<01100110>        ->        output port 2 (code for "4")
<01000000>        ->        output port 1
                  wait 1 msec
<00000000>        ->        output port 1
<01001111>        ->        output port 2 (code for "3")
<00100000>        ->        output port 1
                  wait 1 msec
<00000000>        ->        output port 1
<01011011>        ->        output port 2 (code for "2")
<00010000>        ->        output port 1
                  wait 1 msec
<00000000>        ->        output port 1
<00000110>        ->        output port 2 (code for "1")
<00001000>        ->        output port 1
                  wait 1 msec
<00000000>        ->        output port 1
<00111111>        ->        output port 2 (code for "0")
<00000100>        ->        output port 1
                  wait 1 msec
<00000000>        ->        output port 1
```

Figure 3.13 7-segment driving sequence to display "543210"

inputs and which are outputs. Each of the data direction
register bits is set to 0 if the corresponding line is to be
an input and 1 if it is to be an output. For example, if the
data direction register held <01010011> then lines L7, L5,
L3, and L2 in Figure 3.14 would be inputs while L6, L4, L1
and L0 would be outputs. The data direction register can be
written by the processor at any time.

Figure 3.14 shows three registers within the interface
device. Each can be read or written by the processor. When
the data register is written, the bits in it which correspond
to outputs appear on their respective lines. When it is
read, the states of those lines which are configured as
inputs appear in their respective bits. The control and
status register, when written, affects the functioning of the
device and the state of the extra output bit shown in the
figure. When read, it gives the status of the interface and
of the extra input bit. These two extra bits can be used for
a variety of purposes, including handshaking of data with the
input/output device connected to the interface. The
functions of the control and status register can be

Communicating with microcomputers

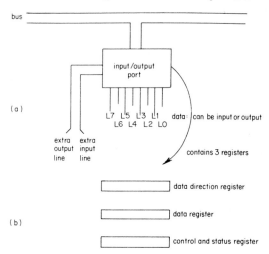

Figure 3.14 Combining input-output in the same port
(a) Configuration
(b) Registers within the interface

summarized as:

[write]   set/reset extra output bit
          enable/disable handshaking
          select data direction register or data register
          enable/disable interrupts
              (i.e. should the processor be informed
              automatically when new data is present?)

[read]   read extra input bit
          read interrupt status
              (i.e. is new data present?)

The Appendix to this chapter discusses manufacturer's technical literature on one commercially-available interface device, the Motorola PIA, which contains two separate 8-bit input/output ports.

SERIAL TRANSMISSION

As mentioned earlier, serial transmission is used with remote devices. The data rate will be relatively low, because cramming all the data down one wire is inherently slower than using a parallel connection with many wires. Such devices are usually character-oriented input/output

terminals, such as teletypes, VDUs (visual display units),
and printers. Serial transmission can either be
"synchronous" or "asynchronous", depending on whether the
receiving and transmitting devices are driven by a common
clock. We will examine the protocol for asynchronous
transmission only.

According to a standard convention, transmission of a
serial data word is preceded by a "start bit" and terminated
by one or two "stop bits". Start bits are LOW and stop bits
are HIGH, so a HIGH-to-LOW transition is guaranteed at the
beginning of a start bit. This transition signals to the
receiver that a data word is coming. The receiver and the
transmitter will have clocks running at approximately the
same rates, but because no clock line is included in the
cable joining the devices, they will not be synchronized
together. The start bit allows the receiver to get its clock
into synchronization. Then, the line state is examined in
the middle of each data bit. The stop bits give time for the
receiver to ready itself for the next word. Figure 3.15
shows the bits transmitted for the data word <01001000>.

Of course, if the receiver gets out of synchronization,
for example by being switched on in the middle of a data
word, it may mistake a HIGH-to-LOW transition between data
bits for the beginning of the start bit. Then the first word
would be misread. The same mistake could also occur
subsequently; however, there is a good chance that
synchronization will be regained within the first few words.
Figure 3.16 shows how start and stop bits can be mis-
identified, and indeed the first four data words received are

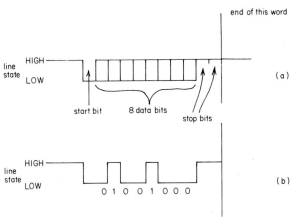

Figure 3.15 (a) Serial transmission of an 8-bit word
           (b) Serial transmission of the word 01001000

garbled. The fifth and subsequent ones, however, are received correctly.

The number of bits/second transmitted down the line is called the "bit rate" or "data rate". (You may come across the expression "baud rate", a technical term used with telecommunications systems. For the kind of transmission we are considering, the baud rate happens to be the same as the bit rate. However, the definition of a "baud" involves extra complications that are not relevant here.) If 2 stop bits and 8 data bits are used, the bit rate is 11 times the rate of characters per second. Typical bit rates are:

transmitted words

01001000   01100101   01101100   01101100   01101111   00101110

transmitted bits
    (start and stop bits marked by ^ and _ respectively)

...111100 100 1000 1100 1100 1011 100 110 1100 1100 110 1100 1100 1101111
     ___^ | _^   _^   _^   _^
                |
                | 11000 101110 111...
                | ^
                | _^   ___
                |
                |
     receiver switched
        on here

received start and stop bits

1000 1100 1100 1011 100 110 1100 1100 110 1100 1100 1101111
 _^   ??_^   _^   _^   ___

                              11000 101110 111...
                                  ^
                                 _^   ___

received words

00110011   11100110   01100110   01100110   00101110

Figure 3.16 Regaining synchronization with asynchronous
            transmission

teletype	110 bits/sec	10 chars/sec
VDU	9600 bits/sec	960 chars/sec
printer	1200 bits/sec	120 chars/sec

Note that the higher data-rate devices use only 1 stop bit. The reason for this is that two stop bits are needed to allow mechanical teleprinters to recover between characters, while faster all-electronic devices, like the VDU's described in the next chapter, do not need this leeway.

So far, the principle of serial data transmission has been described. In practice there are various differences which often confuse people trying to set up a serial link. Figure 3.17 summarizes them. We have already seen the alternatives of 1 or 2 stop bits. Similarly, there are different standards for the number of data bits used, of which 7 and 8 bits are the commonest. 7 bits (128 symbols) are ample to encode the alphabet, while for transmission of data words, 8 bits are more convenient. In either case an extra bit, called the "parity bit", can be added to make the parity (number of 1's in the transmission) even or odd, as an error-detection feature, so 8 or 9 information bits are actually transmitted. There are many standard data rates, of which some of the most common are shown in the figure. Finally, there are different electrical standards for driving the line.

If you work out the combinations in Figure 3.17 you will find over 150 different possibilities. No wonder then, that if you connect a VDU to a serial line it usually doesn't work first time!

A commonly-used standard for coding alphabetic characters into 7-bit words is the ASCII (American Standard Code for Information Interchange) code, shown in Figure 3.18. The ASCII characters include upper- and lower-case letters,

stop bits   data bits   parity   bit rate   electrical

stop bits	data bits	parity	bit rate	electrical
			110	
			300	
1	7	odd	600	voltage driven
			1200	
2	8	even	2400	current driven—20 mA
			4800	＼60 mA
			9600	

Figure 3.17 Some of the options for serial transmission

0000000	nul	0000001	soh	0000010	stx	0000011	etx
0000100	eot	0000101	enq	0000110	ack	0000111	bel
0001000	bs	0001001	ht	0001010	nl	0001011	vt
0001100	np	0001101	cr	0001110	so	0001111	si
0010000	dle	0010001	dc1	0010010	dc2	0010011	dc3
0010100	dc4	0010101	nak	0010110	syn	0010111	etb
0011000	can	0011001	em	0011010	sub	0011011	esc
0011100	fs	0011101	gs	0011110	rs	0011111	us
0100000	sp	0100001	!	0100010	"	0100011	#
0100100	$	0100101	%	0100110	&	0100111	'
0101000	(	0101001	)	0101010	*	0101011	+
0101100	,	0101101	-	0101110	.	0101111	/
0110000	0	0110001	1	0110010	2	0110011	3
0110100	4	0110101	5	0110110	6	0110111	7
0111000	8	0111001	9	0111010	:	0111011	;
0111100	<	0111101	=	0111110	>	0111111	?
1000000	@	1000001	A	1000010	B	1000011	C
1000100	D	1000101	E	1000110	F	1000111	G
1001000	H	1001001	I	1001010	J	1001011	K
1001100	L	1001101	M	1001110	N	1001111	O
1010000	P	1010001	Q	1010010	R	1010011	S
1010100	T	1010101	U	1010110	V	1010111	W
1011000	X	1011001	Y	1011010	Z	1011011	[
1011100	\	1011101	]	1011110	^	1011111	_
1100000	`	1100001	a	1100010	b	1100011	c
1100100	d	1100101	e	1100110	f	1100111	g
1101000	h	1101001	i	1101010	j	1101011	k
1101100	l	1101101	m	1101110	n	1101111	o
1110000	p	1110001	q	1110010	r	1110011	s
1110100	t	1110101	u	1110110	v	1110111	w
1111000	x	1111001	y	1111010	z	1111011	{
1111100	|	1111101	}	1111110	~	1111111	del

Figure 3.18 ASCII codes

numerals, special symbols, and a sprinkling of extra control
codes with standard interpretations like "ht" (assists in
formatting tables — horizontally tabulating — by moving the
printing position along), "bel" (rings the bell on the
terminal), and "etx" (end of transmission). These make the
number of codes up to 128.

SERIAL INTERFACES

Parallel-to-serial and serial-to-parallel conversion is
accomplished by a device called a UART — universal

asynchronous receiver/transmitter. The block diagram of Figure 3.19 shows that the UART is divided into two subsystems, the transmitter and the receiver. The transmitter accepts eight parallel data bits together with five parallel control bits. After they have been latched in the parallel register, the data bits are transferred to the transmitter shift register and shifted out one by one to the serial output. The control bits select some of the options which were discussed earlier in the section on serial devices. The data rate is determined by the transmitter clock.

The receiver subsystem is the complement of the transmitter. Bits from the serial line are shifted in to the receiver shift register. When the data word is complete, the format is checked for parity errors and framing errors (stop bits not encountered when expected), and the word is transferred in parallel to the holding register. "Data available" shows that a new word has been received, and "read data word" reads it out of the device. If the latter has not been asserted by the time the next word is received, the previous word is lost when the new one is transferred to the holding register. In this case the "over-run error" bit is set.

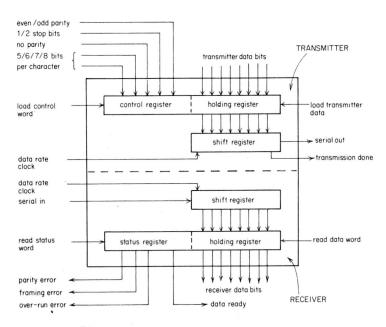

Figure 3.19 UART block diagram

The UART as described makes a perfectly good
serial/parallel converter for microcomputer use. However,
with its plethora of inputs and outputs, it is not
particularly convenient for interfacing to the bus. Special
UARTs, often called ACIAs (asynchronous communications
interface adapters), are manufactured specifically for
microcomputer use. With these, the control and status
information is addressed as a single word, with a read from
it returning the status information and a write setting the
control bits. The "transmission done" signal is included as
a status bit, and some synchronization facilities added.
Similarly, the transmitter and receiver data are combined
into the same register as far as the bus is concerned. All
outputs will, of course, be tri-state so that they can be
connected directly to the bus.

SYNCHRONIZATION OF INTERFACES

Being a connection between one information representation
and another, an interface needs to take account not only of
the information conversion itself but also of the timing
relationship between the devices on either side of it. If
the interface is for input to the microprocessor, the times
at which new information appears are generally unpredictable.
Even on output, times are often unpredictable: if the
throttle position of a car is controlled, the time it takes
to perform an action will depend on various factors not all
of which can be quantified accurately, like the size of the
movement, the condition of the linkage, maybe even
whereabouts in the engine's firing cycle the movement is
initiated. It may well be undesirable to initiate a new
action before the old one is complete. In general we must
consider the processes on either side of the interface to be
asynchronous — and it is usually easiest to treat them as
such even in cases where times can be predicted.

Flags

One way of synchronizing processes is to have a 1-bit
register or "flag" which can be set by one process when it is
finished and cleared by the other. The "ready" line in the
A/D converter of Figure 3.7 could be used to set such a flag.
Then, if the processor wishes to synchronize with the A/D, it
will wait until the ready flag becomes set, then read the
data values and clear the flag. The action of clearing the

flag could well activate the "start" line to begin another
conversion. In this way the processes will be synchronized
in the same manner as a fully-interlocked bus.
Many input interfaces are not as simple as this. With the
A/D, the processor can hold up conversion of the next sample
as long as necessary by refusing to activate the start line.
In the case of a keyboard with hardware debouncing, the user
will press keys when he wants without waiting for a ready
signal from the processor. Here, however, the rate of key-
pressing cannot be very high, partly because people cannot
press buttons quickly and partly because of the mechanics of
the switch itself. Even so, there is a critical time within
which the keyboard must be serviced if input is not to be
missed, and because of this the device is termed real-time.
Another example of a real-time device is the paper-detector
of the printing press in Figure 3.8: the interface must be
serviced in less time than it takes for two flight-bars to
pass the photodiodes.

To guarantee that a real-time interface is serviced within
its critical period, the processor is usually programmed to
repeatedly test the flag to see if it has been set. Once it
has, the processor services the interface (usually by reading
data from it or writing to it), clears the flag, and resumes
its watching vigil. If it has to do some other task, it can
— provided it resumes the watch within the critical time of
the interface. Writing such a real-time program is messy and
error-prone, since the addition of just a few instructions
can throw out the synchronization.

Interrupts

A better synchronization technique is for the interface to
inform the processor when it becomes ready in a more active
way than by setting a flag. A special line, the interrupt
line, is added to the bus for this purpose. This is
electrically similar to the bus request line in that it may
be activated by any of a number of asynchronous devices;
however it does not cause re-allocation of the bus but merely
provides a signal to the processor. If the processor does
not have control of the bus at the time, it will not be able
to do anything about the interrupt — and so other bus
masters should not hog the bus for more than the critical
period of the fastest device (less the time required for the
processor to service the interrupt). If the processor is
currently the bus master it must identify the source of the
interrupt, possibly by explicitly addressing each of the

devices and ascertaining the state of its flag, although
faster techniques exist where the interface device places its
identifying address on some of the bus lines at the request
of the processor.

DIRECT MEMORY ACCESS

All the interfaces we have considered so far are connected
to the bus in the same way as the simple output port of
Figure 3.11. In terms of the bus of Figure 3.20, the
communication is between an input/output device and the
processor, with the processor acting as bus master.
However, one of the reasons for using a bus in the first
place is to allow possibilities for direct communication
between devices other than the processor, particularly
between peripheral devices and the store. This is called DMA
(direct memory access) communication, and to accomplish it
the device interface must take over bus mastership,
temporarily, from the processor.
Figure 3.21 shows an A/D converter with a DMA interface.
At each clock tick, the analogue voltage is converted to
digital and passed to the interface. The task of the
interface is to transfer the value to an appropriate place in
store (i.e. to an appropriate bus address). To do this, it
contains an address register which holds the address where
the next value is to be placed. The address register is
incremented after each "write" operation, so that successive
values are stored in successive store locations. If this
went on for ever, all of store (including any programs) would
eventually be over-written, and so there is a word count
register in the interface which counts words to go, and the
contents of this are decremented after each store operation.
When it becomes zero, the transfers stop. Thus the task of
the interface is to transmit a block of data from the A/D
converter into store. The initial value of the word count

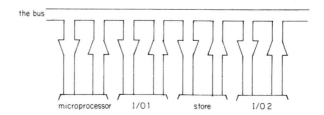

Figure 3.20 Bus-centred computer model

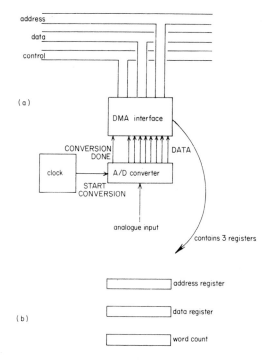

Figure 3.21 A/D converter with a DMA interface
(a) Configuration
(b) Registers within the interface

governs the length of the block, while the initial value of
the address register determines which store locations are
used.

Although the transfers proceed independently of the
processor, it sets the initial values of the address register
and word count. These registers have bus addresses, so that
they are accessible to the processor as normal store
locations. To initiate a DMA operation, the processor writes
appropriate values into the two registers. As soon as the
word count is set non-zero, the interface steps into action,
and thereafter the operation proceeds autonomously, without
bothering the processor. There must, of course, be some way
of signalling to the processor when the operation is
finished. For example, it could find out for itself by
reading the word count register, and waiting until it becomes
zero.

While the word count is non-zero, the interface monitors
the "conversion done" line from the A/D converter. When this
is asserted, it transfers the A/D output into the data

register and then proceeds to request bus mastership. As
described in the last chapter (Figure 2.24), this involves
quite a complicated protocol, using the bus request, bus
busy, and bus grant lines. Once mastership is granted, the
interface puts the contents of its address and data registers
on to the address and data bus, operates "read/write", and
enters the handshaking sequence with the store by asserting
"address valid". When handshaking is complete, it
relinquishes the bus by releasing "bus busy" and the transfer
is done. Now it decrements its local address register,
decrements the word count register, and if this is still
non-zero begins the whole operation again.

SUMMARY

     Computer subsystems can be divided into those that can
initiate transfers on the bus and those that can't. The
former will become bus master on occasion, while the latter
will not and so can ignore the whole problem of bus
contention, including the bus request, bus busy, and bus
grant lines. Simple input/output devices only respond to
processor requests and so are of the second type, while to
transfer data directly from an input/output device to the
store the device must be able to handle the bus-mastership
protocol.
     Another important distinction is between devices that use
parallel data transmission and those that use serial
transmission. In the former there are several wires
(typically 8), one to carry each of the data bits. In the
latter, only one wire is used and the data bits follow each
other along it. Serial transmission is used when the path
from the bus interface to the device itself is quite long and
the device does not accept or generate data at a high rate
(less than, say, 10000 or 20000 bits/sec). Parallel
transmission is used for fast devices, or for devices which
reside physically close to the bus. A multitude of
miscellaneous devices like lights and switches, A/D and D/A
converters, are generally connected in parallel to
interfaces, whereas serial transmission is usually used for
character-oriented devices like VDUs.
     Driving lights is complicated by the problem of refresh.
Although the data can be latched at the peripheral device, it
is often cheaper if there are many lights to refresh them
repeatedly from the processor to create an illusion of
continuous illumination without latching. A loosely
analogous problem with switches and keyboards is that of

debouncing. These problems can be solved either with hardware (data latching, or debouncing circuits) or with software (refreshing, or imposing a delay in the program after a change of state), and illustrate nicely the trade-off, typical of microcomputer systems, between software and hardware complexity.

A/D and D/A converters, and lights and switches, are parallel devices. Even so, interfacing them to a parallel bus is usually done with the help of an interface chip which handles the control lines, latches and buffers the data, and accomodates interrupts.

The major difficulty with serial transmission is mastering the various combinations of options that are part of all serial interface standards. Interface chips exist to handle the basic serial/parallel conversion and the formatting bits (start, stop, and parity).

FURTHER READING

Leventhal, L.A. (1978) "Introduction to Microprocessors: Software, Hardware, Programming." Prentice Hall, Englewood Cliffs, New Jersey.
> This is a good all-round introductory book on microprocessor hardware and programming. Chapter 8 covers input-output, and Chapter 9 treats interrupt systems in considerably more detail than we do here. By coincidence, Leventhal also describes the Motorola PIA which is the subject of the Appendix of the present chapter; and so if you have difficulty with the data sheets in the Appendix, this is where to look for help.

Mansfield, P.H. (1973) "Electrical Transducers for Industrial Measurement." Butterworths, London.
> Although not a microprocessor-oriented book at all, this describes the principles of all sorts of conversions between different information representations.

Millman, J. & Halkias, C.C. (1972) "Integrated Electronics." McGraw Hill, Tokyo.
> Sections 17-19 and 17-20 of this comprehensive electronics text describe D/A and A/D conversion, in considerably more detail than we have seen in this chapter.

Osborne, A. (1977) "An Introduction to Microprocessors Volume
  2 — Some Real Products." Adam Osborne and Associates,
  Berkeley.
    Gives manufacturer's data on a whole range of
    input and output interfaces — PIA's, VIA's,
    PIO's, MILE's, etc..

Peatman, J.B. (1977) "Microcomputer-based Design." McGraw
  Hill, New York.
    In Chapter 5, Peatman describes quite a lot of
    different commercially-available interface
    devices, and shows how they can be connected to
    the bus.

APPENDIX: THE MOTOROLA PIA

    The pages that follow give manufacturer's technical
literature on the Motorola PIA, which contains two separate
8-bit parallel ports (port A and port B). It is quite
complicated, and you will probably not understand it all, but
it is as well that you should know just how complicated
manufacturer's literature can be! In fact, this is a
relatively _simple_ device: there is another, the MOS
Technology VIA, which has 16 registers and is more complex
than many processor chips!
    Here are some suggestions for studying the information.
It will probably take an hour or two, with paper and pencil.

1. Read the introductory paragraph to see roughly what the
    chip does.
2. Examine the pin assignments given on the last page.
3. List the signals, grouped according to their acronyms
    (PA0-PA7, D0-D7, ...).
4. Try to guess what each group of signals is for. (Use
    Figure 3.14, remembering that there are two eight-bit
    ports.)
5. Check your guesses thoroughly by reading the
    descriptions on the second page. (Ignore the interrupt
    facilities for now.)
6. Discover what internal registers are provided which can
    be read or written from the processor.
7. Consider how six internal registers are addresses by
    only two register-select pins (what is the "Control
    register bit" of Table 1?).
8. If you wish, try to ascertain what interrupt facilities
    are provided, and what CA1, CA2, CB1, CB2 are (Tables 3,

4 and 5). This is difficult.
9. Discover the differences between Port A and Port B.
10. Draw your own block diagram of the interface, after the
    manner of Figure 3.14. Annotate the diagram with pin
    numbers and the function of the control and status
    register bits.
11. Draw a circuit to interface an 8-bit A/D and D/A to the
    bus, using a PIA at bus addresses <1111111111110000> to
    <1111111111110011>.

MANUFACTURER'S TECHNICAL LITERATURE

PERIPHERAL INTERFACE ADAPTER (PIA)

The MC6820 Peripheral Interface Adapter provides the universal
means of interfacing peripheral equipment to the MC6800 Micro-
processing Unit (MPU). This device is capable of interfacing the MPU
to peripherals through two 8-bit bidirectional peripheral data
buses and four control lines. No external logic is required for interfacing to
most peripheral devices.

The functional configuration of the PIA is programmed by the
MPU during system initialization. Each of the peripheral data lines
can be programmed to act as an input or output, and each of the
four control/interrupt lines may be programmed for one of several
control modes. This allows a high degree of flexibility in the over-all
operation of the interface.

- 8-Bit Bidirectional Data Bus for Communication with the MPU
- Two Bidirectional 8-Bit Buses for Interface to Peripherals
- Two Programmable Control Registers
- Two Programmable Data Direction Registers
- Four Individually-Controlled Interrupt Input Lines; Two Usable
  as Peripheral Control Outputs
- Handshake Control Logic for Input and Output Peripheral
  Operation
- High-Impedance 3-State and Direct Transistor Drive Peripheral
  Lines
- Program Controlled Interrupt and Interrupt Disable Capability
- CMOS Drive Capability on Side A Peripheral Lines

MC6820

PERIPHERAL INTERFACE
ADAPTER

L SUFFIX
CERAMIC PACKAGE
CASE 715

NOT SHOWN: P SUFFIX

PLASTIC PACKAGE
CASE 711

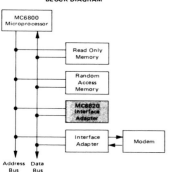

M6800 MICROCOMPUTER FAMILY
BLOCK DIAGRAM

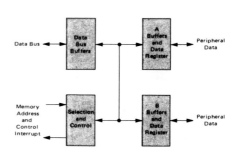

MC6820 PERIPHERAL INTERFACE ADAPTER
BLOCK DIAGRAM

PIA INTERFACE SIGNALS FOR MPU

The PIA interfaces to the MC6800 MPU with an eight-bit bi-directional data bus, three chip select lines, two register select lines, two interrupt request lines, read/write line, enable line and reset line. These signals, in conjunction with the MC6800 VMA output, permit the MPU to have complete control over the PIA. VMA should be utilized in conjunction with an MPU address line into a chip select of the PIA.

PIA Bi-Directional Data (D0-D7) — The bi-directional data lines (D0-D7) allow the transfer of data between the MPU and the PIA. The data bus output drivers are three-state devices that remain in the high-impedance (off) state except when the MPU performs a PIA read operation. The Read/Write line is in the Read (high) state when the PIA is selected for a Read operation.

PIA Enable (E) — The enable pulse, E, is the only timing signal that is supplied to the PIA. Timing of all other signals is referenced to the leading and trailing edges of the E pulse. This signal will normally be a derivative of the MC6800 φ2 Clock.

PIA Read/Write (R/W) — This signal is generated by the MPU to control the direction of data transfers on the Data Bus. A low state on the PIA Read/Write line enables the input buffers and data is transferred from the MPU to the PIA on the E signal if the device has been selected. A high on the Read/Write line sets up the PIA for a transfer of data to the bus. The PIA output buffers are enabled when the proper address and the enable pulse E are present.

$\overline{\text{Reset}}$ — The active low $\overline{\text{Reset}}$ line is used to reset all register bits in the PIA to a logical zero (low). This line can be used as a power-on reset and as a master reset during system operation.

PIA Chip Select (CS0, CS1 and $\overline{\text{CS2}}$) — These three input signals are used to select the PIA. CS0 and CS1 must be high and $\overline{\text{CS2}}$ must be low for selection of the device. Data transfers are then performed under the control of the Enable and Read/Write signals. The chip select lines must be stable for the duration of the E pulse. The device is deselected when any of the chip selects are in the inactive state.

PIA Register Select (RS0 and RS1) — The two register select lines are used to select the various registers inside the PIA. These two lines are used in conjunction with internal Control Registers to select a particular register that is to be written or read.

The register and chip select lines should be stable for the duration of the E pulse while in the read or write cycle.

Interrupt Request ($\overline{\text{IRQA}}$ and $\overline{\text{IRQB}}$) — The active low Interrupt Request lines ($\overline{\text{IRQA}}$ and $\overline{\text{IRQB}}$) act to interrupt the MPU either directly or through interrupt priority circuitry. These lines are "open drain" (no load device on the chip). This permits all interrupt request lines to be tied together in a wire-OR configuration.

Each Interrupt Request line has two internal interrupt flag bits that can cause the Interrupt Request line to go low. Each flag bit is associated with a particular peripheral interrupt line. Also four interrupt enable bits are provided in the PIA which may be used to inhibit a particular interrupt from a peripheral device.

Servicing an interrupt by the MPU may be accomplished by a software routine that, on a prioritized basis, sequentially reads and tests the two control registers in each PIA for interrupt flag bits that are set.

The interrupt flags are cleared (zeroed) as a result of an

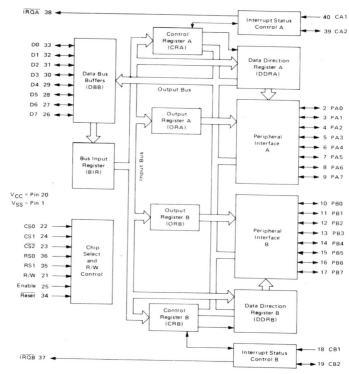

MPU Read Peripheral Data Operation of the corresponding data register. After being cleared, the interrupt flag bit cannot be enabled to be set until the PIA is deselected during an E pulse. The E pulse is used to condition the interrupt control lines (CA1, CA2, CB1, CB2). When these lines are used as interrupt inputs at least one E

pulse must occur from the inacti e edge to the active edge of the interrupt input signal to condition the edge sense network. If the interrupt flag has been enabled and the edge sense circuit has been properly conditioned, the interrupt flag will be set on the next active transition of the interrupt input pin.

PIA PERIPHERAL INTERFACE LINES

The PIA provides two 8-bit bi-directional data buses and four interrupt/control lines for interfacing to peripheral devices.

Section A Peripheral Data (PA0-PA7) — Each of the peripheral data lines can be programmed to act as an input or output. This is accomplished by setting a "1" in the corresponding Data Direction Register bit for those lines which are to be outputs. A "0" in a bit of the Data Direction Register causes the corresponding peripheral data line to act as an input. During an MPU Read Peripheral Data Operation, the data on peripheral lines programmed to act as inputs appears directly on the corresponding MPU Data Bus lines. In the input mode the internal pullup resistor on these lines represents a maximum of one standard TTL load.

The data in Output Register A will appear on the data lines that are programmed to be outputs. A logical "1" written into the register will cause a "high" on the corresponding data line while a "0" results in a "low". Data in Output Register A may be read by an MPU "Read Peripheral Data A" operation when the corresponding lines are programmed as outputs. This data will be read properly if the voltage on the peripheral data lines is greater than 2.0 volts for a logic "1" output and less than 0.8 volt for a logic "0" output. Loading the output lines such that the voltage on these lines does not reach full voltage causes the data transferred into the MPU on a Read operation to differ from that contained in the respective bit of Output Register A.

Section B Peripheral Data (PB0-PB7) — The peripheral data lines in the B Section of the PIA can be programmed to act as either inputs or outputs in a similar manner to PA0-PA7. However, the output buffers driving these lines differ from those driving lines PA0-PA7. They have three-

state capability, allowing them to enter a high impedance state when the peripheral data line is used as an input. In addition, data on the peripheral data lines PB0-PB7 will be read properly from those lines programmed as outputs even if the voltages are below 2.0 volts for a "high". As outputs, these lines are compatible with standard TTL and may also be used as a source of up to 1 milliampere at 1.5 volts to directly drive the base of a transistor switch.

Interrupt Input (CA1 and CB1) — Peripheral Input lines CA1 and CB1 are input only lines that set the interrupt flags of the control registers. The active transition for these signals is also programmed by the two control registers.

Peripheral Control (CA2) — The peripheral control line CA2 can be programmed to act as an interrupt input or as a peripheral control output. As an output, this line is compatible with standard TTL; as an input the internal pullup resistor on this line represents one standard TTL load. The function of this signal line is programmed with Control Register A.

Peripheral Control (CB2) — Peripheral Control line CB2 may also be programmed to act as an interrupt input or peripheral control output. As an input, this line has high input impedance and is compatible with standard TTL. As an output it is compatible with standard TTL and may also be used as a source of up to 1 milliampere at 1.5 volts to directly drive the base of a transistor switch. This line is programmed by Control Register B.

NOTE: It is recommended that the control lines (CA1, CA2, CB1, CB2) should be held in a logic 1 state when Reset is active to prevent setting of corresponding interrupt flags in the control register when Reset goes to an inactive state. Subsequent to Reset going inactive, a read of the data registers may be used to clear any undesired interrupt flags.

INTERNAL CONTROLS

There are six locations within the PIA accessible to the MPU data bus: two Peripheral Registers, two Data Direction Registers, and two Control Registers. Selection of these locations is controlled by the RS0 and RS1 inputs together with bit 2 in the Control Register, as shown in Table 1.

DATA DIRECTION REGISTERS (DDRA and DDRB)

The two Data Direction Registers allow the MPU to control the direction of data through each corresponding peripheral data line. A Data Direction Register bit set at "0" configures the corresponding peripheral data line as an input; a "1" results in an output.

CONTROL REGISTERS (CRA and CRB)

The two Control Registers (CRA and CRB) allow the MPU to control the operation of the four peripheral control lines CA1, CA2, CB1 and CB2. In addition they allow the MPU to enable the interrupt lines and monitor the status of the interrupt flags. Bits 0 through 5 of the two registers may be written or read by the MPU when the proper chip select and register select signals are applied. Bits 6 and 7 of the two registers are read only and are modified by external interrupts occurring on control lines CA1, CA2, CB1 or CB2. The format of the control words is shown in Table 2.

TABLE 1 — INTERNAL ADDRESSING

RS1	RS0	CRA-2	CRB-2	Location Selected
0	0	1	X	Peripheral Register A
0	0	0	X	Data Direction Register A
0	1	X	X	Control Register A
1	0	X	1	Peripheral Register B
1	0	X	0	Data Direction Register B
1	1	X	X	Control Register B

X = Don't Care

INITIALIZATION

A low reset line has the effect of zeroing all PIA registers. This will set PA0-PA7, PB0-PB7, CA2 and CB2 as inputs, and all interrupts disabled. The PIA must be configured during the restart program which follows the reset.

Details of possible configurations of the Data Direction and Control Register are as follows.

TABLE 2 — CONTROL WORD FORMAT

	7	6	5	4	3	2	1	0
CRA	IRQA1	IRQA2	CA2 Control			DDRA Access	CA1 Control	

	7	6	5	4	3	2	1	0
CRB	IRQB1	IRQB2	CB2 Control			DDRB Access	CB1 Control	

Data Direction Access Control Bit (CRA-2 and CRB-2) — Bit 2 in each Control register (CRA and CRB) allows selection of either a Peripheral Interface Register or the Data Direction Register when the proper register select signals are applied to RS0 and RS1.

Interrupt Flags (CRA-6, CRA-7, CRB-6, and CRB-7) — The four interrupt flag bits are set by active transitions of signals on the four Interrupt and Peripheral Control lines when those lines are programmed to be inputs. These bits cannot be set directly from the MPU Data Bus and are reset indirectly by a Read Peripheral Data Operation on the appropriate section.

TABLE 3 — CONTROL OF INTERRUPT INPUTS CA1 AND CB1

CRA-1 (CRB-1)	CRA-0 (CRB-0)	Interrupt Input CA1 (CB1)	Interrupt Flag CRA-7 (CRB-7)	MPU Interrupt Request IRQA (IRQB)
0	0	↓ Active	Set high on ↓ of CA1 (CB1)	Disabled — IRQ remains high
0	1	↓ Active	Set high on ↓ of CA1 (CB1)	Goes low when the interrupt flag bit CRA-7 (CRB-7) goes high
1	0	↑ Active	Set high on ↑ of CA1 (CB1)	Disabled — IRQ remains high
1	1	↑ Active	Set high on ↑ of CA1 (CB1)	Goes low when the interrupt flag bit CRA-7 (CRB-7) goes high

Notes:
1. ↑ indicates positive transition (low to high)
2. ↓ indicates negative transition (high to low)
3. The Interrupt flag bit CRA-7 is cleared by an MPU Read of the A Data Register, and CRB-7 is cleared by an MPU Read of the B Data Register.
4. If CRA-0 (CRB-0) is low when an interrupt occurs (Interrupt disabled) and is later brought high, IRQA (IRQB) occurs after CRA-0 (CRB-0) is written to a "one".

Control of CA1 and CB1 Interrupt Input Lines (CRA-0, CRB-0, CRA-1, and CRB-1) — The two lowest order bits of the control registers are used to control the interrupt input lines CA1 and CB1. Bits CRA-0 and CRB-0 are used to enable the MPU interrupt signals IRQA and IRQB, respectively. Bits CRA-1 and CRB-1 determine the active transition of the interrupt input signals CA1 and CB1 (Table 3).

TABLE 4 — CONTROL OF CA2 AND CB2 AS INTERRUPT INPUTS CRA5 (CRB5) is low

CRA-5 (CRB-5)	CRA-4 (CRB-4)	CRA-3 (CRB-3)	Interrupt Input CA2 (CB2)	Interrupt Flag CRA-6 (CRB-6)	MPU Interrupt Request IRQA (IRQB)
0	0	0	↓ Active	Set high on ↓ of CA2 (CB2)	Disabled — IRQ remains high
0	0	1	↓ Active	Set high on ↓ of CA2 (CB2)	Goes low when the interrupt flag bit CRA-6 (CRB-6) goes high
0	1	0	↑ Active	Set high on ↑ of CA2 (CB2)	Disabled — IRQ remains high
0	1	1	↑ Active	Set high on ↑ of CA2 (CB2)	Goes low when the interrupt flag bit CRA-6 (CRB-6) goes high

Notes:
1. ↑ indicates positive transition (low to high)
2. ↓ indicates negative transition (high to low)
3. The Interrupt flag bit CRA-6 is cleared by an MPU Read of the A Data Register and CRB-6 is cleared by an MPU Read of the B Data Register.
4. If CRA-3 (CRB-3) is low when an interrupt occurs (Interrupt disabled) and is later brought high, IRQA (IRQB) occurs after CRA-3 (CRB-3) is written to a "one".

TABLE 5 — CONTROL OF CB2 AS AN OUTPUT CRB-5 is high

CRB-5	CRB-4	CRB-3	CB2 Cleared	CB2 Set
1	0	0	Low on the positive transition of the first E pulse following an MPU Write "B" Data Register operation.	High when the interrupt flag bit CRB-7 is set by an active transition of the CB1 signal.
1	0	1	Low on the positive transition of the first E pulse after an MPU Write "B" Data Register operation.	High on the positive edge of the first "E" pulse following an "E" pulse which occurred while the part was deselected.
1	1	0	Low when CRB-3 goes low as a result of an MPU Write in Control Register "B".	Always low as long as CRB-3 is low. Will go high on an MPU Write in Control Register "B" that changes CRB-3 to "one".
1	1	1	Always high as long as CRB-3 is high. Will be cleared when an MPU Write Control Register "B" results in clearing CRB-3 to "zero".	High when CRB-3 goes high as a result of an MPU Write into Control Register "B".

Control of CA2 and CB2 Peripheral Control Lines (CRA-3, CRA-4, CRA-5, CRB-3, CRB-4, and CRB-5) — Bits 3, 4, and 5 of the two control registers are used to control the CA2 and CB2 Peripheral Control lines. These bits determine if the control lines will be an interrupt input or an output control signal. If bit CRA-5 (CRB-5) is low, CA2 (CB2) is an interrupt input line similar to CA1 (CB1) (Table 4). When CRA-5 (CRB-5) is high, CA2 (CB2) becomes an output signal that may be used to control peripheral data transfers. When in the output mode, CA2 and CB2 have slightly different characteristics (Tables 5 and 6).

TABLE 6 — CONTROL OF CA-2 AS AN OUTPUT
CRA-5 is high

CRA-5	CRA-4	CRA-3	CA2 Cleared	CA2 Set
1	0	0	Low on negative transition of E after an MPU Read "A" Data operation.	High when the interrupt flag bit CRA-7 is set by an active transition of the CA1 signal.
1	0	1	Low on negative transition of E after an MPU Read "A" Data operation.	High on the negative edge of the first "E" pulse which occurs during a deselect.
1	1	0	Low when CRA-3 goes low as a result of an MPU Write to Control Register "A".	Always low as long as CRA-3 is low. Will go high on an MPU Write to Control Register "A" that changes CRA-3 to "one".
1	1	1	Always high as long as CRA-3 is high. Will be cleared on an MPU Write to Control Register "A" that clears CRA-3 to a "zero".	High when CRA-3 goes high as a result of an MPU Write to Control Register "A".

PIN ASSIGNMENT

1	Vss	CA1	40
2	PA0	CA2	39
3	PA1	IRQA	38
4	PA2	IRQB	37
5	PA3	RS0	36
6	PA4	RS1	35
7	PA5	Reset	34
8	PA6	D0	33
9	PA7	D1	32
10	PB0	D2	31
11	PB1	D3	30
12	PB2	D4	29
13	PB3	D5	28
14	PB4	D6	27
15	PB5	D7	26
16	PB6	E	25
17	PB7	CS1	24
18	CB1	CS2	23
19	CB2	CS0	22
20	Vcc	R/W	21

PACKAGE DIMENSIONS

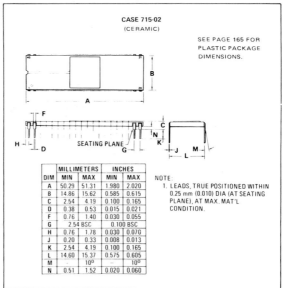

CASE 715-02
(CERAMIC)

SEE PAGE 165 FOR PLASTIC PACKAGE DIMENSIONS.

DIM	MILLIMETERS MIN	MILLIMETERS MAX	INCHES MIN	INCHES MAX
A	50.29	51.31	1.980	2.020
B	14.86	15.62	0.585	0.615
C	2.54	4.19	0.100	0.165
D	0.38	0.53	0.015	0.021
F	0.76	1.40	0.030	0.055
G	2.54 BSC		0.100 BSC	
H	0.76	1.78	0.030	0.070
J	0.20	0.33	0.008	0.013
K	2.54	4.19	0.100	0.165
L	14.60	15.37	0.575	0.605
M	—	10^0	—	10^0
N	0.51	1.52	0.020	0.060

NOTE:
1. LEADS, TRUE POSITIONED WITHIN 0.25 mm (0.010) DIA (AT SEATING PLANE), AT MAX. MAT'L CONDITION.

Graphical Communication

Pictures are a venerable, a natural, and often a most
effective way of communicating information, and can greatly
enhance a dialogue between man and machine. On the simplest
level, functional or empirical relationships can be displayed
as a computer-generated plot, and as an example some trend
curves for the stock market, together with the individual
stock prices on which they are based, are shown in Figure
4.1. Rather more exciting is the representation of three-

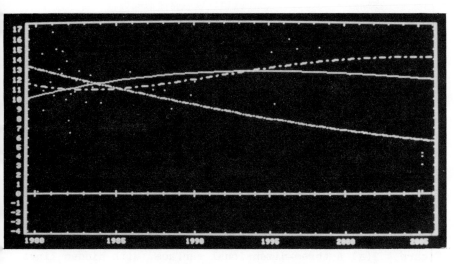

Figure 4.1 Stock prices, with trend curves

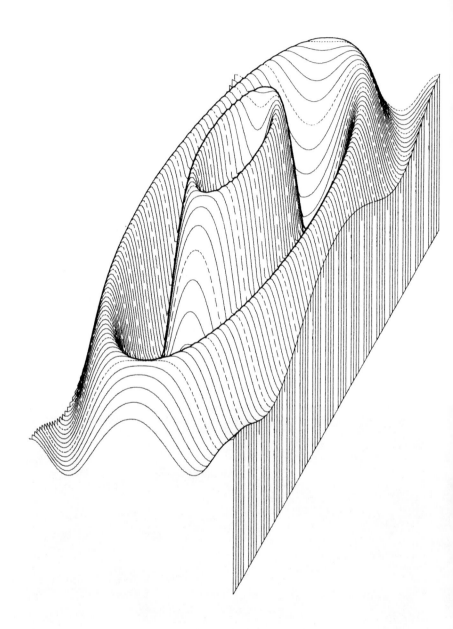

Figure 4.2(a) A three-dimensional surface, with hidden lines
            removed

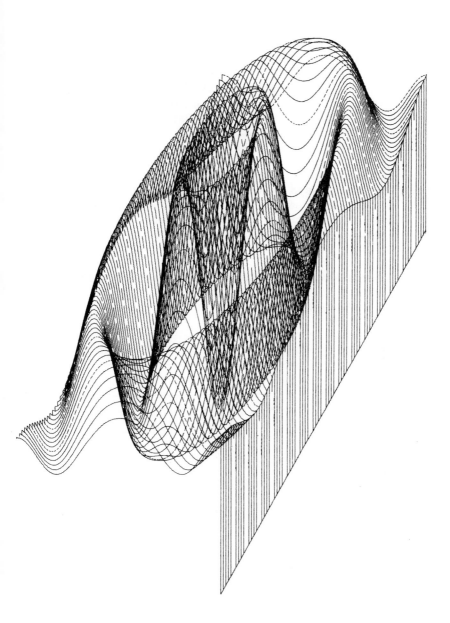

Figure 4.2(b) The same surface with all lines visible

dimensional surfaces like the one in Figure 4.2(a) of a
mathematical function. Notice that "hidden lines" have been
removed from this picture by the computer — the same
function is plotted in Figure 4.2(b) with all lines visible.
Another use for line drawings is electrical circuit diagrams
(Figure 4.3). Here the computer can perform analysis of the
circuit as well as simply drawing it, probably presenting the
results of this as electrical waveforms expected at key test
points. Since circuits are often etched directly on the
surface of a printed circuit board using a photographic
process, this too can be automated.

The display of text itself is a most important application
of computer graphics, and Figure 4.4 shows a typical VDU
(visual display unit) computer terminal. Text can be
presented in new ways which are impossible on paper, for
parts of the screen may be dynamically overwritten, or
highlighted by blinking. Suitable software can restrict any
input typed on the keyboard to pre-defined parts of the page,
for example to assist with filling in a questionnaire. On
the other hand the VDU can be very constraining — annotating
a text or scoring out sections is often much easier on paper.
A large variety of type fonts can be accommodated, and Figure
4.5 shows a VDU which can display Chinese text.

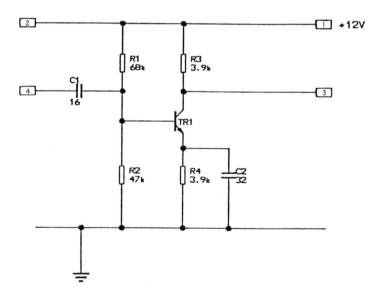

Figure 4.3 Electrical circuit diagram

Figure 4.4 VDU computer terminal

Limited graphics capability is provided in many microcomputer display systems, like that used in the teletext facility of the British television services and also in the viewdata scheme (promoted by the Post Office under the name "Prestel"). This generates low-resolution pictures of the type shown in Figure 4.6, which are particularly effective in colour. On home computers, such facilities are usually designed to enhance computer games.

Much more expensive equipment is needed to draw three-dimensional shaded objects, and here the computational burden of hidden-line removal can become very great. The illusion of depth is greatly enhanced by the ability to change the apparent viewing position by rotating the object: this too places heavy demands on both the display hardware and supporting software. Systems exist which provide a cockpit view from a simulated aeroplane, allowing you to bank and loop, swoop low over roads and fields, land, and taxi across the airfield into a hangar!

Graphical input is much more primitive. Of course you can interface a television camera to a computer bus and digitize visual images, but interpreting them with a program is currently a challenging research problem. The effects of lighting and shadow, which at first seem to confound recognition by tarnishing and confusing the objects which are being viewed, are in fact important, but subtle, clues to shape and orientation in real-world scenes. Further complications arise from binocular vision, and motion of the object or observer. Even two-dimensional line drawings

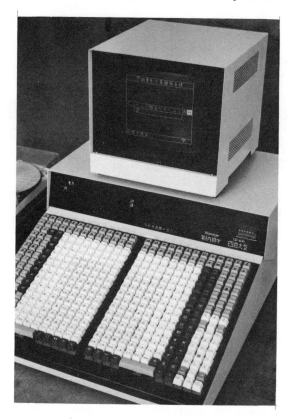

Figure 4.5 Chinese VDU

present considerable difficulties. The thumbnail sketch
which so greatly assists communication between engineers or
architects is virtually impossible to interpret
automatically. Of course, it is easy to <u>record</u> such pictures
by computer, and they can be processed by scale changes or
rotation and stored for subsequent output on demand — the
difficulty is in deducing facts about the structure of the
objects depicted. While recording and replaying pictures can
be most useful for mediating communication between one person
and another, the emphasis of this book is on man-<u>computer</u>
communication, and for this it is necessary for the machine
to interpret its input.
     The easiest thing to interpret is pointing — and this can
be put to extraordinarily good use. It is well suited to the
machine's capacity for high-speed display, and to man's
potential for rapid assimilation of pictorial information,
quick decision-making, but rather restricted output

Figure 4.6 A teletext weather map

capability. This leads to the use of a "menu" to show
possible options which are selected by pointing; to a stylus
which can "pick up" part of a picture and "drag" it around
the screen; to "rubber-band lines" which extend from a point
on the screen to the stylus tip and move around with it,
keeping straight all the time. All these facilities can be
provided by a display and suitable software if only the pen
coordinates are continually known.

This chapter introduces the technology of interactive
computer graphics. The "interactive" qualifier is important
here because it excludes displays which cannot be used for
quickly-changing pictures. For example, a plotter which
draws lines on paper with a computer-controlled pen is not
considered interactive, for it produces pictures slowly, one
at a time. In fact once you appreciate the principles of
interactive displays, non-interactive ones are easy to
handle. We begin with graphical output, covering two
fundamental techniques of random point-plotting and raster-
scanning. Although random point-plotting is the oldest and
still the dominant technique for high-quality graphics, it is
being ousted by raster-scanning, particularly in mass-
produced low-cost systems. Hence we spend rather more time
on the latter, discussing the generation of characters,
cell-organized raster displays, and related graphics
facilities like those of the teletext and viewdata systems.
Then, two devices for input are described, one of which is
inherently a pointing device while the other is not but can
be made so by suitable software. Finally we look at a new

input peripheral which recognizes hand-printing, to give a
taste of things to come.

POINT-PLOTTING DISPLAYS

Let's consider the simplest kind of display. It needs to
be able to position a spot on the face of a screen by
controlling its x and y coordinates. Think of an
oscilloscope, where x and y deflection mechanisms steer the
beam of light to any position on application of suitable
control voltages. The details of the deflection mechanism
itself are not important for an understanding of the
potential of the display for man-machine interaction; however
certain properties of it do affect the kind of pictures that
can be drawn and the cost of the display, and we will come to
these in a moment. In addition to x and y control, a z or
brightness-control is needed to turn the spot on and off.
Figure 4.7 shows how the display can be connected to the
computer bus. Three output ports are provided, one for each
of the beam's degrees of freedom. D/A converters change the
digital x and y coordinates to voltages which control the
deflection mechanism, while since the brightness is either on
or off, only a buffer is needed to provide two suitable
voltage levels. (This buffer is really a 1-bit D/A
converter!) The resolution that is required of the
converters depends on the accuracy with which the position
has to be specified. Typically, 10-bit converters are used,
giving a grid of 1024 x 1024 points. Notice that this grid
contains a total of just over one million points, and if each
can be on or off then there are over $2^{1000000}$ possible

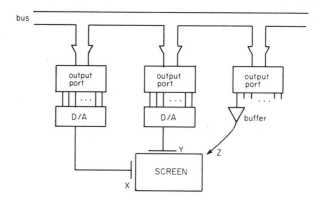

Figure 4.7 Connecting a point-plotting display to the bus

patterns that can be displayed. This is a truly enormous
number, whose decimal representation has more than 300,000
digits, and the old adage that a picture is worth a thousand
words is clearly an underestimate!

Part of a program for driving the display is shown below.
This presents a spot at the point with coordinates (52,716).
Can you see why the program manipulates z and does not just
leave it at 1 all the time? Physical considerations of the
display hardware may dictate some changes in the program. It
may be necessary to wait between steps 4 and 5 to give the
spot time to brighten up, and between 3 and 4 to allow the
position of the beam to settle.

Refresh

What happens when the program is executed once? The spot
will move to the specified point, brighten up, and that will
be that. If you're lucky you might catch a glimpse of a
brief and microscopic flash on the face of the screen. To
give an illusion of a sustained point, the display needs to
be refreshed periodically, every 20 msec or so, just as the
LED's were at the beginning of the last chapter. The refresh
rate required depends on the properties of the display
itself: usually light is produced by an electron beam
striking a phosphor-coated screen and the duration of the
spot depends on the "persistence" of the phosphor used. The
need to refresh brings many problems in the design and use of
computer displays, because if several thousand points are to
be refreshed every 20 msec there is not much time for each!
— for a 1024 x 1024 display contains over a million points.
If the display is not refreshed quickly enough the picture
will flicker: this begins to become noticeable at a refresh
rate of about 30 Hz (33 msec between refreshes).

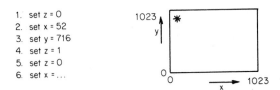

Figure 4.8 Part of a program to drive the display

Timing Considerations

Important parameters of a point-plotting system are:

D/A conversion time
deflection speed of the beam
attack time of the phosphor
persistence of the phosphor
refresh rate
computer speed.

A typical settling time for D/A converters is 1 or 2 usec.
The currents in the bank of resistors described in the last
chapter must stabilize, and after the operational amplifier
sums these its output voltage must settle. High-speed D/A
converters can be built to stabilize after as short a time as
30 nsec. The deflection speed of the beam depends on the
deflection system used. There are two important ones,
magnetic and electrostatic deflection, the former taking as
long as 25 usec for a corner-to-corner movement of the beam
and the latter accomplishing even this large movement in 1
usec. Why not always use electrostatic deflection? — it
costs more! The magnetic scheme is used in television
receivers, and these are available very cheaply because of
their high sales volumes. The attack time of the phosphor
causes no difficulty, being of the order of 50 nsec. Its
persistence varies depending on the type of phosphor used.
While long persistence — and it can be as long as several
seconds — means that the refresh rate can be lower, it
prevents rapid changing of the display contents because
after-images of the old picture remain on the screen. This
is quite distracting, and so persistences of around 5 to 10
msec are used for interactive displays, allowing a refresh
rate of 25-50 Hz to be employed without after-images.
Finally, if the computer is used in a simple point-plotting
mode as indicated in Figures 4.7 and 4.8, the program
execution time to display one point will be 30-100 usec on
present-day microprocessors.
   With a refresh rate of 25 Hz and a 40 usec point-plotting
time, only 1000 points can be displayed on the screen. This
is just 0.1% of the total number of points, and corresponds
to a single full-length line. If characters are to be
displayed and each has 20 points, then only 50 of them can be
accommodated — less than a line of text. Clearly computer
speed is the big limitation.

FROM INTERFACE TO DISPLAY PROCESSOR

The scheme of Figure 4.7 requires the processor to pick up the coordinates of each point from store and send them along the bus to the display interface. A DMA arrangement can substantially increase the speed, with the interface gaining bus mastership and reading the coordinates from store without intervention by the processor. Then, the speed of the bus-mastership protocol becomes the limiting factor, unless the display interface hogs the bus for substantial periods by refusing to relinquish bus mastership once it has been granted. This in turn can prevent the processor from operating at a reasonable speed.

Figure 4.9 shows a solution which uses a dual-port store. The display interface has private access to the store along a special display bus, and transfers on this do not interfere with the main bus or with the processor's operation. Of course, the store must arbitrate between simultaneous read or write requests from the two ports. In general, the processor will have another store on the main bus which it uses unless it specifically requires to update the display: then the processor and the display interface can each work at full speed quite independently.

Now what is the limitation on our display system's performance? Coordinates can be retrieved from the store very quickly — 500 nsec is a typical store access time. 1 usec D/A converters will keep up with this, since two coordinates must be read for every point displayed. However, the 25 usec corner-to-corner deflection offered by a typical magnetic system will not, and this will severely restrict the images that can be displayed unless the points are arranged in the store in a way that minimizes large jumps.

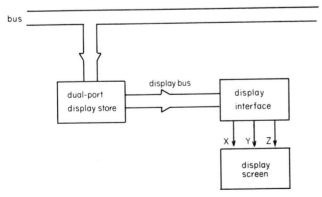

Figure 4.9 A display scheme with a dual-port store

Furthermore, when large jumps do occur the display interface
must detect them and wait for a suitable period for the beam
to settle. An electrostatic display eliminates the need for
this and provide a far more satisfactory, but expensive,
solution.

More serious limitations are the size of the display
store, and the time it takes the processor to write a picture
to it. A thousand points need 2000 coordinate
specifications. Thus even a large 64 Kword store will only
accommodate 32 full length lines. And the processor will
take a correspondingly long time to change the picture in the
display store, so to avoid a muddled display during the
change a second 64 Kword store will be needed, with a
switching arrangement to allow the display to change over
instantaneously from one picture to another (a technique
known as "double-buffering").

It is worth considering adding line-generating hardware to
compute the intermediate points of a straight line from its
beginning and end coordinates. Such hardware interpolates in
a straight line from the beginning x voltage to the final
one, and similarly for the y voltage (see Figure 4.10). This
is not difficult to implement in either analogue or digital
hardware, although there are trade-offs between the two which
we will not go into. The Appendix to this chapter describes
one digital line-drawing algorithm which can be implemented
in hardware or software. The display interface must

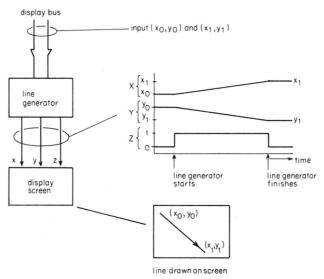

Figure 4.10 Operation of a line generator

distinguish commands to the line generator from x,y
coordinate specifications of individual points, and one or
more bits must be reserved for this purpose with every data
item in the display store. Now the display interface becomes
more like a processor in its own right, interpreting
instructions in the display store, and in fact is usually
called a "display processor" (Figure 4.11).

What other tasks would it be nice for the display
processor to do? It could have circle generators, ellipse
generators, and so on. If characters are to be shown then a
special hardware character generator is useful, for it is
extremely wasteful of store to specify a character as a set
of points each time it is to be displayed. We will discuss
character generators in another section. It could do
windowing of data, allowing the display store to contain a
picture larger than that actually drawn on the screen.
Rotation of pictures is also possible. Rotation in two
dimensions is accomplished by the coordinate change

$$x' = x \cos theta + y \sin theta$$
$$y' = x \sin theta - y \cos theta,$$

where theta is the angle of rotation, and since this
transformation needs to be done on all points it is rather
slow unless special facilities are provided in hardware.
(Note, however, that if a hardware line generator is used the
rotation transformation need only be done on the end-points
of lines.) Three-dimensional rotation is almost as easy, and
can be combined with perspective transformations to provide
viewing of an object from any position. This brings in
hidden-line suppression and shading, which can also be done
by the display processor. A subroutining facility is useful
too, for it is often convenient to define a component of a
picture (like a house) once and regenerate it from the same
description at various places on the screen.

Now the display processor, which started as a simple
interface, has become quite a sophisticated piece of
hardware, much more complicated than the average
microprocessor. It needs an expensive electrostatic display
screen with an impressive array of intricate supporting
hardware. The exploitation of such sophisticated displays
for man-machine interaction is a specialist topic in its own
right. Let us climb down a little and look and less
expensive, and less powerful, display techniques.

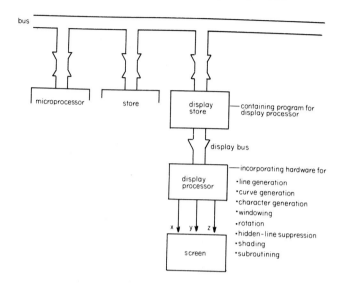

Figure 4.11 Display processor

RASTER-SCAN DISPLAYS

The picture on a domestic television is painted by scanning across from left to right on the screen, one line after another, from top to bottom. The technique is known as "raster-scanning". It places relatively light demands on the deflection system of the tube, for the flyback time from the end of each line to begin the next and the frame flyback time across the diagonal of the screen are known and picture information is not broadcast during these periods. Hence a cheap magnetic deflection mechanism can be used, and this, along with the economies of large-scale production, accounts for the low cost of domestic TV sets. To reduce flicker, two successive rasters are displayed, each one generating alternate lines in an interlaced fashion as shown in Figure 4.12. One raster is transmitted every 20 msec and so the complete picture is redrawn in 40 msec. This rather low refresh rate of 25 Hz does not cause noticeable flicker so long as the pictures on the two rasters are similar — as they always are in TV transmissions.

In Britain the screen size is nominally 625 lines, some of which are lost in the frame flyback time. If interlace is ignored the number of lines is halved, giving around 290 on the screen. Rounding this down to a power of 2 and assuming a square picture, a screen size of 256 x 256 is obtained — a quarter the resolution of the high-quality displays described

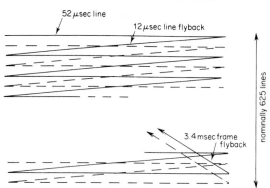

Figure 4.12 Television raster-scan, with interlace

in tne previous section. It is possible to double the number
of lines on tne screen by taking interlace into account, but
this may increase flicker to an intolerable level, because
unlike the case of normal TV transmission the interlaced
pictures are significantly different.

If a single bit is stored for each point to indicate
whether it is bright or not, each line needs 32 bytes of
storage and the full screen needs 8 Kbyte. If this resides
in the computer's main store then the result is the memory-
mapped bit-per-point display system of Figure 4.13. The
operation of the scan-generator interface between the store
and the TV set is quite simple. Each of the 32 bytes in a
line is read in sequence at the appropriate time and its bits
used to modulate the beam intensity. Notice that the store
is a dual-port one, but the line and frame flybacks provide
periods when the processor can access it without contention.
In contrast with the point-plotting display, it is easy to
brighten up whole areas of the screen, for a point occupies
the same fraction of the raster whether it is white or black.
There is no limitation on the total length of lines which can
be drawn.

As always, however, there are problems. For example, to
display a line between point (32,255) and point (0,240) you
must set bit 4 of word 4, bit 6 of word 36, bit 1 of word 67,
bit 3 of word 99, and so on, as shown in the figure. This
can take rather a long time to calculate. And characters are
just as time-consuming: imagine the bits that would have to
be changed in Figure 4.14 to move a page of text up one line!
So while memory-mapped oit-per-point displays are certainly
flexible they are not at all convenient to use. Furthermore,
to take advantage of the grey-scale possibilities afforded by
TV, where there are several shades of grey between white and

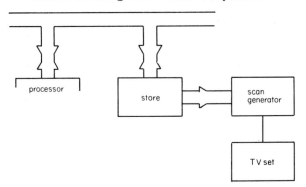

Figure 4.13 Memory-mapped bit-per-point display system

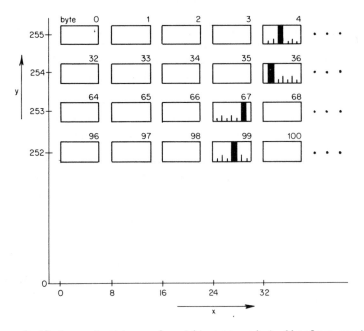

Figure 4.14 Organization of a bit-per-point display system

black, several bits must be reserved for each point,
multiplying the size of store needed. This goes for colour
as well, of course.

CELL-ORGANIZED DISPLAYS

To make a display system easily manageable by the programs
that generate the pictures, it is necessary to impose a

structure on them that allows the raw picture data to be
compressed and stored in a meaningful way. For example, we
saw earlier how line-generating hardware in a point-plotting
display processor permits a whole line to be given just by
its two end points. The natural structure to impose on a
raster-scanned display is a pattern of rectangular cells.
Figure 4.15 shows a 256 x 256 bit-per-point screen organized
as a 32 x 32 array of cells, each one being 8 x 8 dots.
There are 64 bits in each cell, so 2^{64} possible patterns can
occupy one cell alone. However, most of these patterns are
unlikely to be used in a simple picture. Suppose we
sacrifice flexibility for convenience and low cost by
defining a small repertoire — say 256 — of patterns which
may occupy each cell. Then to hold the complete set of
patterns we need 256 x 8 x 8 bits = 2 Kbyte, and now a
particular pattern can be indicated by an 8-bit pattern
number. Since there are 32 x 32 cells on the screen, only
1024 of these numbers, or 1 Kbyte, are needed to hold the
screen contents (Figure 4.16).

This certainly saves some storage. Previously, 8 Kbyte
was needed to hold the screen contents on a bit-per-point
basis. Now only 1 Kbyte specifies the screen contents,
together with 2 Kbyte for the pattern dictionary. The price
paid is heavy, though: only a tiny fraction of possible
pictures can be displayed. But the real advantage is one of
convenience: now the computer need only wrestle with a 32 x

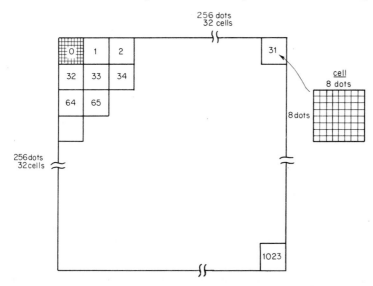

Figure 4.15 Cell-organized display with 1024 8 x 8 cells

32 array of cells instead of a 256 x 256 array of dots.
Since its storage and bus structure is in terms of bytes and
not bits anyway, it is actually easier to handle cell pattern
numbers than individual dots. (Recall the difficulty of
generating straight lines on a bit-per-point display.)

Figure 4.17 shows the connection of a memory-mapped cell-
organized display to the computer bus. As with the bit-per-
point system of Figure 4.13, the display system is called
"memory-mapped" because the screen contents appear to the
processor as ordinary store. The connection between the bus
and the pattern dictionary is dashed because it is often not
there at all: the patterns are fixed and cannot be changed
by the processor.

The success of a cell-organized display in practice
depends on the match between the patterns in the cells and
the kind of pictures that are drawn on the screen. General
cell displays which are intended for line drawings have been
built: here the cell repertoire naturally consists of line
segments. However, the number of possible line segments
through an 8 x 8 dot cell is unreasonably large, and
rotational and axial symmetry is called into play to reduce
the dictionary size. Then, the display interface must be
able to perform rotation and symmetry transformations, and
becomes a display processor which treats the screen contents
store more as a program than as a list of pattern numbers.
This parallels precisely the development of the display
processor for point-plotting displays.

Let us instead examine some rather less ambitious pattern
repertoires for cell-organized displays.

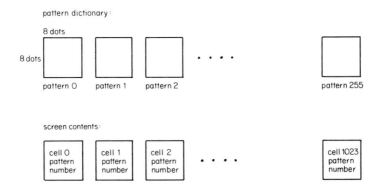

Figure 4.16 Pattern dictionary and screen contents for
cell-organized display

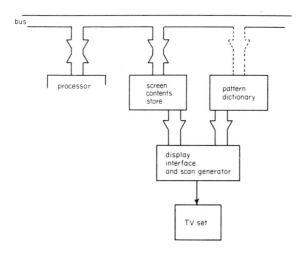

Figure 4.17 Memory-mapped cell-organized display

CHARACTER GENERATION

One obvious use for a cell-organized display is to show
text. Cell-organized character displays are called VDU's
(visual display units) — a rather unfortunate term because
it gives no indication that only characters can be shown.
The screen of Figure 4.15 can accommodate 32 lines of 32
characters, each one being on an 8 x 8 grid. Of course,
space must be left between neighbouring characters and
between successive lines, so the actual character area is
normally chosen as 7 x 5 dots.

Character Storage

A 7 x 5 dot matrix is quite adequate for upper-case
characters, digits, and some special symbols. The standard
64-character upper-case alphabet is shown in Figure 4.18,
along with the characters that augment it to the standard
96-character upper-and-lower-case alphabet. Although lower-
case characters can be written satisfactorily on a 7 x 5
matrix, five of them — g, j, p, q, and y — have tails which
should descend below the line if written properly. This
needs a 9 x 5 dot matrix, with any one character occupying
either the upper or the lower 7 x 5 section; this works
because there aren't any characters with both descenders and
"risers". Higher-quality text can be obtained with an 11 x 7
matrix, with any given character occupying either the upper

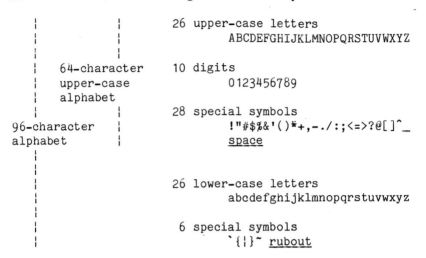

Figure 4.18 Standard 64-character and 96-character alphabets

or the lower 9 x 7 section. The possibilities are summarized
in Figure 4.19, where a dotted outline shows the cell
containing the character, including inter-character and
inter-line space, and the solid line shows the actual size of
the characters.

Read-only memory chips with the character patterns already
in them are available from a variety of manufacturers. A
typical specification is shown in Figure 4.20. When
addressed with the ASCII code of a character, the appropriate
dot pattern appears on the output pins. Actually, the
address of a particular row of dots is usually provided to
the character generator as well, and the dots comprising only
that row appear on the output pins. Thus with 64 characters
of 7 x 5 dots each, 9 bits are required to address a
particular row of a character and there are 5 output pins
giving the dots in that row. This arrangement is especially
suited to raster-scan displays, because one line of the
raster is generated at a time. Note that for character
generators like that in Figure 4.20, the action of "lowering"
characters with descenders must be done externally to the
chip, the user providing circuitry to detect these five
characters and adjust the row address accordingly.

The amount of storage required in a character generator is
quite small. For our example, we need 512 words of 5 bits to
provide the 64-character upper-case alphabet.

A 256 x 256 screen accommodates 32 lines of 32 characters
if the character cell is 8 x 8, 21 lines of 42 characters if
it is 12 x 6, and only 17 lines of 28 characters if it is 15

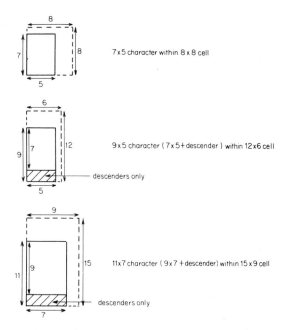

7x5 character within 8x8 cell

9x5 character (7x5+descender) within 12x6 cell

descenders only

11x7 character (9x7 +descender) within 15x9 cell

descenders only

Figure 4.19 Common character sizes

x 9. All of these sizes are unrealistically small for text.
A normal sheet of typed paper can comfortably hold about 57
lines of 80 characters. To achieve this with a 12 x 6 cell
would require a 684 x 480 screen, which is not possible
within the British 625-line standard. Many VDU's compromise
with about 24 full-length lines of 80 characters, requiring a
288 x 480 screen. There is currently a great deal of
commercial interest in high-quality VDU's, and special high-
resolution screens are built for them — but they don't have
the advantage of the mass TV market to bring down the price.
However, it is worth noting that a 1125-line high-resolution
TV system is under development in Japan, which should
accommodate up to 75 lines of high-quality text with a 11 x 7
character size (15 x 9 cell).

The VDU

VDU's are not, in general, memory-mapped. It is far more
convenient for the computer user to regard his text as a
linear string, sending it one character at a time to the
display device. Usually it is transmitted in serial form by
a parallel-to-serial converter attached to the bus, as shown

MOS
LSI

TMS 2501 JC, NC
64 x 5 x 7 STATIC USASCII CHARACTER GENERATOR

MAY 1975

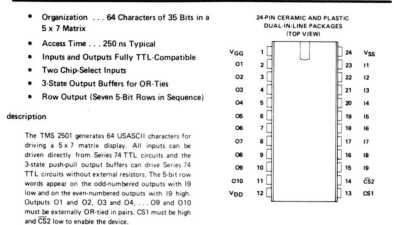

- Organization . . . 64 Characters of 35 Bits in a 5 x 7 Matrix
- Access Time . . . 250 ns Typical
- Inputs and Outputs Fully TTL-Compatible
- Two Chip-Select Inputs
- 3-State Output Buffers for OR-Ties
- Row Output (Seven 5-Bit Rows in Sequence)

description

The TMS 2501 generates 64 USASCII characters for driving a 5 x 7 matrix display. All inputs can be driven directly from Series 74 TTL circuits and the 3-state push-pull output buffers can drive Series 74 TTL circuits without external resistors. The 5-bit row words appear on the odd-numbered outputs with I9 low and on the even-numbered outputs with I9 high. Outputs O1 and O2, O3 and O4, . . . O9 and O10 must be externally OR-tied in pairs. CS1 must be high and $\overline{CS2}$ low to enable the device.

The TMS 2501 is offered in 24-pin ceramic (JC suffix) or plastic (NC suffix) packages designed for insertion in mounting-hole rows on 600-mil centers. The devices are characterized for operation from $-25°$C to 85°C.

functional block diagram

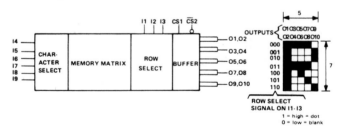

Figure 4.20 Specification of a character-generating read-only memory

in Figure 4.21. The VDU must provide store for the screen contents, but this only needs one byte per character displayed — say 2 Kbyte for 24 lines by 80 characters. In fact, local storage is sometimes provided for a good deal more than this, so that the VDU can retain several screenfuls of text and you can look back to see what was presented a few moments ago.

The VDU itself has to decide what to do when the screen fills up. A scrolling feature is almost universally provided, where the entire screen contents move up as

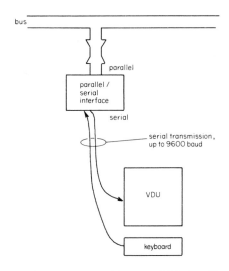

Figure 4.21 Connecting a VDU to the bus

necessary. Continual rapid jumping of the text is irritating
and tiring for the reader, and so several lines are scrolled
at a time. Smooth scrolling, where the contents move up a
dot at a time rather than jumping whole lines is
unfortunately rather rare at present, although it does not
cause any particular technical problems. Other features
which are often provided are blinking of the text on a
selected area of screen, reverse video (black text on a white
background), half-intensity or double-intensity display, and
underlining of parts of the text. These options are switched
on and off by control characters (ASCII codes 0000000 -
0011111) sent down the line as part of the text — which can
unfortunately alter all subsequent characters if a text
character is corrupted by noise into a control character!
    One really useful feature is the ability to move the
current position for text to any point on the screen, so that
characters in the middle of the text can be overwritten. A
mark called the "cursor" is usually made on the screen at the
current writing position, and any input typed on the keyboard
appears at the cursor position (which is moved along with
each successive character). Then, a questionnaire can be
displayed and the cursor moved to the places where the user
enters his answers, constraining him to write in the space
provided. Cursor control is again dictated by a special
character which signals the VDU to interpret the next
character as the cursor position. Notice that this
reinstates the flexibility of a memory-mapped display where a

character can be placed at any position on the screen.
    Most VDU's operate at speeds up to 9600 baud. Unlike
printers, no extra effort is needed to make a VDU go fast.
9600 baud allows a full screen of 24 x 80 characters to be
sent in 2 seconds, which is certainly a high reading rate!
However, people often <u>scan</u> text much faster than this — how
quickly do you read a newspaper? Present VDU technology
leaves plenty of room for improvement.

LIMITED GRAPHICS

    Pressure to provide limited graphics facilities based on
inexpensive raster-scanned displays has come from two
directions: home computers and the teletext and viewdata
information services. The character-generating read-only
memories of most home computers contain an assortment of
graphic symbols to draw primitive pictures. Figure 4.22, for
example, shows the 64 symbols of PET, a typical low-priced
domestic computer. In order that graphic symbols can abut to
form pictures, the inter-word and inter-character spaces are
stored explicitly in the character generator and not provided
by external hardware as in most VDU's. PET uses an 8 x 8

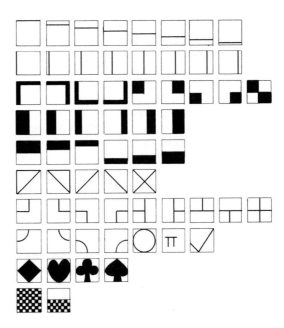

Figure 4.22 PET graphic symbols

cell. The standard 64-character upper-case alphabet of
Figure 4.18 is provided, together with the 64 graphic symbols
or the lower-case letters — software can select which of
these latter groups is used. Some of the graphics reflect
the game-playing orientation of PET; but the lack of coherent
structure of the others makes constructing pictures or charts
a rather tedious task. There is no standardization of
graphics alphabets in the home computer industry.

Teletext

The teletext scheme for broadcast information defines a
graphics standard, and it is possible that this might spread
to the microcomputer industry. It uses 64 codes in a
systematic way to provide a refinement of its basic 24 x 40
character grid. Each cell is split into the six regions
shown in Figure 4.23, and a 6-bit word specifies any
combination of white and black ones. Thus an effective 72 x
80 grid is available for graphics, and the picture of Figure
4.6 gives an example of the resolution obtained. The
teletext cell is not square but has 10 x 8 dots, with a 9 x 5
upper-and-lower-case character matrix. The problem of
dividing a cell 10 rows high into three equal portions for
the graphic symbols is a continuing challenge for teletext
receiver designers! Teletext also has a defined protocol for
coping with colour displays by inserting colour-change
control characters into the text stream.

User-Defined Graphics

An unusual and interesting limited graphics facility is
provided in the Sorcerer home computer. 256 character codes
are used instead of the usual 64 or 96. Of these, 128

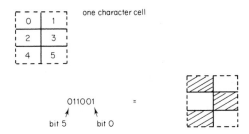

Figure 4.23 Teletext graphics

correspond to pre-defined patterns, which include the
96-character basic alphabet of Figure 4.18 together with 32
extra graphics. For the others, the character-generating
memory can be altered by the processor, so that the user can
define his own graphic symbols. Since the character matrix
is 8 x 8, 8 bytes serve to define one character, and the
read-only and writeable parts of the character generator are
each 1 Kbyte. The circuitry required to generate characters
from a read/write memory is a little more complex than for
read-only memories, because contention will occur when the
display reads and the processor writes simultaneously. But
the extra power provided is enormous, for the Sorcerer can
simulate both PET and the teletext system, as well as others.
For example, graphs can be displayed quite accurately by
defining 8 patterns each with one dot in the centre, at
different heights. Or a character set can be defined for
line drawings which includes all the line segments which are
needed in a particular picture. Or a Cyrillic alphabet for
text in Russian. This combines much of the flexibility of
the memory-mapped bit-per-point display with a structure that
can show text sensibly and simulate systems like PET and
teletext.

THE LIGHT-PEN AND TABLET

The Light-Pen

    Turning now to graphical input, a light-pen is a device
that detects whether or not there is a spot of light on the
screen at the place it is pointing. It can also signal the
exact time the light appears. Recall that the picture is
refreshed every 40 msec or so, so that if the pen points at a
spot which is brightened up a signal will appear during every
refresh cycle. The interrupt mechanism is ideally suited to
advising the processor at the precise time a hit occurs.
    The time-of-hit information provided naturally by a
light-pen can easily be converted into the position of the
hit by adding the hardware shown by dashed lines in Figure
4.24. The x and y signals from the output port are routed
back to an input port — in practice, this will be before
they are converted from digital to analogue form — and
loaded into two registers there whenever a hit occurs. Then
the processor can examine these registers at leisure to
ascertain the position of the last hit.
    But which kind of information, time-of-hit or

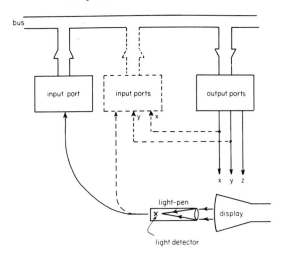

Figure 4.24 Operation of a light-pen

coordinates-of-point, is more useful?   Suppose the house
picture of Figure 4.25 is stored as 28 lines:

    line 1:   beginning x,y   ending x,y
    line 2:   beginning x,y   ending x,y
    .
    .
    .
    line 28:   beginning x,y   ending x,y

and line-generating hardware drives the display.   Then,
although the x,y coordinates of a hit can in theory be used
to determine which line was being drawn, the precise time
when it occurred leads to the information much more easily
because the processor only needs to examine its last request
to the line-generator.   In general, the <u>state</u> <u>of</u> <u>the</u> <u>display</u>
<u>processor</u> at the time of the hit will provide most
information about what was actually being drawn at the time,
not the coordinates of the hit point.

Tracking a Light-Pen

    A light-pen only registers a hit if the spot it is
pointing at is actually brightened up during the refresh
cycle.   If you point it at a blank part of the screen the
processor cannot tell where it is.   A "tracking cross" is
often drawn as part of the picture; this follows the pen

Figure 4.25 A house

around in an attempt to provide light for it to see. For the
cross of Figure 4.26, if a hit occurs on line 1 the cross
should move up, for line 2 it should move to the left, and so
on. The processor detects the hits and moves the cross as
necessary. Because the light-pen actually sees a small area
of the screen rather than a single point, if it moves north-
west then hits will occur on both lines 1 and 2 and the
processor will be able to move the cross appropriately. It
is quite easy to lose the cross by moving the pen quickly,
and when this happens you have to go back to the cross and
"pick it up" again with the pen. If the centre of the cross
coincides with part of the picture, then a hit is registered
whenever that component of the picture is refreshed, and so
the processor can tell what part is being indicated and can
take appropriate action.

The Touch-Tablet

Figure 4.27 illustrates another kind of graphical input
device which is entirely independent of any display and
provides the coordinates of the pen position. Current is
injected into a uniform resistive sheet through the pen tip,
and is measured at one side of the tablet while the other is
earthed. The resistive sheet acts as a potential divider,
and the ratio of the output to the input current gives one
coordinate. Then the connections are changed so that the
other coordinate can be measured.
A particularly interesting feature of the tablet is that a
finger can act as the pen, using high-frequency alternating
current and capacitive coupling with the sheet instead of DC
with direct coupling. Effectively, you sit on an electric
chair and inject current with your finger (but it doesn't
hurt!). Then, no pen is needed and if the sheet is made
transparent and fitted on to a display screen, you can
indicate parts of the picture just by pointing at them with a
finger.
This device provides coordinate information and not time-

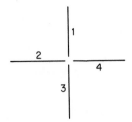

Figure 4.26 Tracking cross

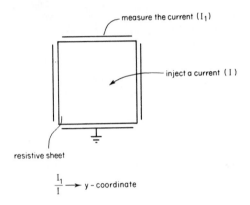

Figure 4.27 An x,y tablet

of-hit. However, it can easily be made into time-of-hit by comparing the x,y coordinates from the tablet with those being sent to the display. When they coincide (to within a specified tolerance), a hit interrupt is caused.

RECOGNIZING ORDINARY HAND-PRINTING

Figure 4.28 shows a new development in graphical input — a device to recognize ordinary hand-printing. As you write with a biro on a paper form, the characters appear on a display above the writing area. If you make a mistake — or, perhaps more likely, the recognizer makes a mistake — you simply re-write the character in the same position. If it cannot be identified a blob appears on the display and you can try again. However, provided you write carefully the recognizer makes few mistakes — perhaps one or two on each form.

Sit back for a moment and think of the uses of such a

Figure 4.28 Micropad: a device that recognizes hand-printing

device. You could write telex messages and have them
transmitted via a computer straight from your desk, with no
intermediaries to make mistakes. A telephone ordering clerk
could write down the orders as they come in over the phone,
and not have to type them on a keyboard. There are many
advantages to this, for she can fill in a form in any order
and not be constrained by the top-to-bottom structure imposed
by a typewriter. (The device sends the position of the
character, along with the code for it, to the central
computer.) You could have one in a Post Office, and enter
money transfers directly into the computer instead of on a
form which is then copied by a clerk — clearly a reliable
signature verifier would be needed as well.
     How is it done? Firstly, unlike the light-pen or tablet
described above, writing is with an ordinary pen. The
writing-pad responds to pressure rather than electrical or
optical connection. In fact, it comprises two sheets of
resistive material separated by a small gap, so that a slight
pressure will make them touch. This completes an electrical
circuit which measures the x,y coordinates by a technique
similar to that of the tablet.
     The coordinates of each point are converted to digital and
transferred straight to the store of a microcomputer system,
using DMA. Then, the program segments the input into
strokes. The fact that timing information is available about

how the character is drawn considerably eases the task of
recognition — it would be much more difficult to recognize
characters from their shapes alone. Figure 4.29 shows the
stroke decomposition of some of the characters. While an "S"
and a "5" often look alike, they are usually drawn in quite a
different way, the "S" being one continuous stroke and the
"5" being three, with a movement of the pen to begin the last
stroke. Similarly, "Z" and "2" differ. There may be more
than one way to draw a character. For example, "Z" can be
barred or unbarred, and "E" can be drawn in two ways: these
possibilities are taken into account by the program. For
each stroke, some features are extracted like its direction,
whether it is curved or not, and what accelerations occur;
and these are used to assist the matching of a drawn
character with a stored example of it.

    Some characters really can be the same, like the letter
"O" and the digit "0"; the letter "I" and the digit "1".
Here, constraints on the dialogue must be used (like whether
the input is a number or a name) to resolve ambiguity.

    The peripheral of Figure 4.28 provides ASCII-coded
characters, each preceded by a byte which indicates its
position, and transmits them using the serial-line convention
described in Chapter 3.

SUMMARY

    Graphical output from computers is a complex trade-off
between speed, storage, processing power, and cost. Point-
plotting displays offer a simple solution which is limited by
the amount of data that can be output by the processor in one
refresh period. Adding a dual-port store, so that the
display interface itself can read coordinates from the store

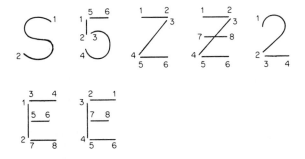

Figure 4.29 Stroke decompositions for characters

without relying on the processor, speeds up the display and many more points can be shown. The limitation now becomes a matter of store size and the difficulty of updating the display without intermediate, muddled, pictures being seen.

Either of two directions can be taken to enhance the display's power. The first is to make the interface a specialist processor in its own right, with real-time line and character generation hardware and other facilities. It executes a program specified by the main processor which describes the picture. Now the problem becomes one of the display-processor complexity — the line and character generators must work quite fast to regenerate an involved picture in real time — and the physics of the display tube. Quick re-positioning of the beam is needed, and this — while possible — is expensive, requiring a special electrostatically-driven display.

The other possibility is to note that if many points are to be shown it is more economical to store them as a binary matrix with one bit for every possible dot on the screen, than as a list of individual coordinates. Furthermore, if the dots are stored in the correct order then a cheap raster-scanned domestic TV set can display them. Now the problem becomes one of deciding on the contents of the display store, and the fixed order in which points are shown complicates the generation of lines and characters. A suitable structure which can be imposed on the store is a cell organization, where one of a small repertoire of possible patterns can appear in any cell and the display store contains for each cell the index number of its pattern. This organization is ideal for VDU's, and special graphics symbols can be added to the repertoire for simple pictures and charts. If the symbols can be re-defined by the user then much of the flexibility of the original bit-per-point system can be regained, within a simple cell structure.

One useful form of graphical input simply allows you to point at a part of the picture. Surprisingly, the precise time at which this part of the picture is refreshed is more useful in identifying where the pen is pointing, in terms of the structure of the picture, than its x,y coordinates. The light-pen provides this timing information naturally, although it can easily be converted to coordinates by extra hardware if desired. However, the light-pen can only detect light if it is there, and so a tracking cross is sometimes generated under it to ensure that it has something to see.

A tablet provides x,y coordinates directly, but these can easily be converted into time-of-hit information by hardware. The coordinates are available even if no part of the

displayed picture appears there. It is possible to dispense
with the pen and point with your finger, using a high-
frequency capacitively coupled system.

There are many fascinating areas of computer graphics
which we have not touched upon. Hidden-line removal
algorithms, which in some cases also produce shading
information, are quite interesting, as is the mathematics
behind perspective and other three-dimensional
transformations. How about "hypertext", a text structure
which does not depend on the linear ordering of ideas but
could allow different aspects of a subject to be written
about and pursued by the reader in directions chosen by him
and not the author — a kind of thesauric encyclopaedia? Or
computer-animated movies, where the artist draws a sequence
of key frames and the machine interpolates between them to
form a continuously changing image? (Walt Disney employed
hordes of junior artists to do this difficult but
intellectually undemanding job.) What influence will
computer graphics have on kinetic art? What can be done in
the way of computer interpretation of real-world visual
images? Imagine special glasses containing TV displays that
present a slightly different picture to each eye to simulate
stereo vision, and the pictures change appropriately as you
turn your head or walk forward! Picture the possibilities.

FURTHER READING

Nelson, T.H. (1974) "Dream Machines — New Freedoms through
    Computer Screens." Ted Nelson, Publisher.
        This is the flip side (yes, literally printed on
        the back) of the "Computer lib" book referred to
        in Chapter 1. Like "Computer lib," it's fast-
        moving, zany, and full of crazy ideas.

Newman, W.M. and Sproull, R.F. (1979) "Principles of
    Interactive Computer Graphics." McGraw Hill, New York.
        This book is the definitive treatise on computer
        graphics. Recently revised from an earlier
        version, it's up-to-date and packed with relevant
        information. It concentrates on the more
        sophisticated (and therefore more expensive)
        techniques for point-plotting displays with
        powerful hardware display controllers, although
        this new edition has a substantial chapter on
        cheaper raster-scanned systems.

Stokes, A.V. (1978) "Viewdata: a Public Information Utility."
    Input Two-Nine, London.
    Stokes describes the Viewdata scheme from a non-
    technical point of view, and gives details of the
    British Post Office's offerings on the Prestel
    system.

Walker, B.S., Gurd, J.R. and Drawneek, E.A. (1975)
    "Interactive Computer Graphics." Edward Arnold, London.
    A less advanced, and less useful, book on
    computer graphics than Newman and Sproull's,
    above.

Winston, P.H. (1975) "The Psychology of Computer Vision."
    McGraw Hill, New York.
    Winston describes current progress on computer
    programs that "understand" pictures — part of
    the field of study known as "artificial
    intelligence".

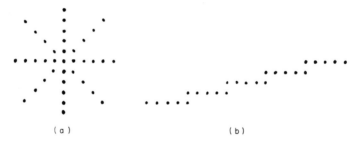

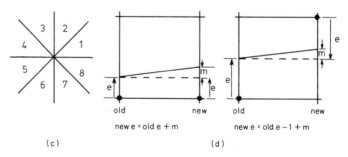

Figure 4.30 Line-drawing on a display
        (a) perfect lines
        (b) jaggies
        (c) octants for the line-drawing algorithm
        (d) the two possibilities for incrementing e

APPENDIX: A LINE-DRAWING ALGORITHM

Although a graphical display comprises discrete points, it
is often used to show continuous line segments. If the line
runs parallel or at 45° to one of the coordinate axes there
is no difficulty: if not, some degree of approximation is
necessary by brightening up points lying near the line. For
lines nearly parallel to the axes, "jaggies" will inevitably
appear as the line moves up from one dot position to the
next. A good line-drawing algorithm will minimize these.

One such algorithm works by keeping a record of the
discrepancy between the last dot which was brightened up and
the actual coordinate of the line. The procedure is slightly
different depending on which of the eight octants of Figure
4.30 the line is in: we will describe it for the first
octant. The x-coordinate is incremented by one for each
point drawn, and the y-coordinate may be incremented
depending on the current value of the discrepancy, e. Figure
4.30(d) shows the two possibilities. If e < 0.5 then y is
not incremented and e is increased by m, the slope of the
line. Otherwise y is incremented and e is adjusted to take
account of the new y-position by subtracting one from it, as
well as increasing it by m. This is described by the program

```
var x,y, x0,y0, x1,y1 : integer;      screen coords are integers
    m, e : real;                      these are real numbers

begin
    m := (y1-y0)/(x1-x0);             calculate the line's slope
    e := 0;                           zero initial discrepancy
    x := x0;  y := y0;
    plot(x,y);                        plot the starting point

    repeat
        if e > 0.5 then begin         if appropriate,
            y := y+1;                 increment y and adjust e
            e := e-1
        end;
        x := x+1;                     x increases by one every
        e := e+m;                     time
        plot(x,y)                     plot the next point
    until x = x1                      carry on until finished

end.
```

Figure 4.31 Pascal line-drawing program

of Figure 4.31, which draws a line between (x0,y0) and
(x1,y1).
 For other octants, the procedure is slightly different.
In octants 4 and 5, x decreases by one every time, instead of
increasing. In octants 5 and 8, y decreases instead of
increasing. In 2, 3, 6, and 7, the roles of x and y are
reversed, y being altered every time and x changing only if e
exceeds 0.5. For these cases, m should be inverted so that
it represents the increase in x per unit y.

Speech Communication

Despite the fact that voice output systems have been
available commercially for several years, the use of speech
for communicating with computers is in its infancy. Existing
systems use direct recording and playback, with either
analogue or digital storage. Clearly, a tape recorder with
an auxiliary addressing mechanism will suffice to generate a
limited number of speech messages, and could be used in a
voice response system if only it were fast and reliable
enough. Commercial devices such as that used for the
speaking clock employ disks or drums with magnetic or optical
storage, the latter using photographic film. Their electro-
mechanical nature makes them cumbersome, expensive, and
inflexible.
　　However, in recent years advances in electronic integrated
circuit technology have provided new voice output devices,
ranging from read-only memories that store a few dozen words
to speech synthesizers capable of simulating the vocal tract
and generating truly synthetic speech. This computer output
medium seems to be on the point of exploding into a fully-
fledged technology in its own right.
　　Synthetic speech output is attractive for many reasons.
Ordinary telephones serve as terminals, and people without
experience of computers are accustomed to their use. A cheap
world-wide distribution network already exists. The touch-
tone keyboard on modern telephones provides a convenient
complementary data input service. Speech synthesis hardware
is becoming available commercially, and the growing interest
in speech output being shown by computer hobbyists, always
eager for new low-cost peripherals, promises to provide a
useful source of expertise in this heretofore rather esoteric

discipline.

It is important to distinguish speech <u>storage</u>, where an actual human utterance is recorded, perhaps processed to lower the data-rate, and stored for subsequent regeneration when required, from speech <u>synthesis</u>, where the machine produces its own individual utterances which are not based on recordings of a person saying the same thing. The difference is summarized in Figure 5.1. In both cases something is stored: for the first it is a direct representation of an actual human utterance, while for the second it is a typed <u>description</u> of the utterance in terms of the sounds, or phonemes, which constitute it. The accent and tone of voice of the human speaker will be apparent in the stored speech output, while for synthetic speech the accent is the machine's and the tone of voice is determined by the synthesis program.

Within speech storage, there is a trade-off between the volume of store that is needed to hold an utterance and the amount of processing required to encode and decode it, and

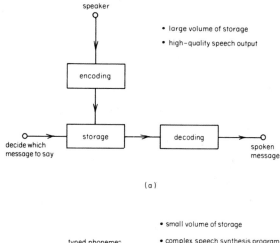

Figure 5.1(a) Speech storage
          (b) Speech synthesis

this is examined in the next section. Even the most compact
encoding consumes an order of magnitude more store than is
required for speech synthesis from a written phonetic
description, for storing phonetics is similar to storing the
English text itself. However, storing a phonetic description
incurs a considerable decrease in intelligibility: speech
synthesis is a young technology and has much progress to
make. Besides, synthesis from phonetics is only part of the
problem, for global aspects of an utterance such as its
rhythm and intonation are not included in a conventional
phonetic transcription but must be communicated somehow to
the speech synthesis program. This is considered next. It
may seem a simple matter to translate from English to
phonetics — after all, just a pronunciation dictionary is
needed — but it is not, and reasons why it is not are
discussed. To round off the subject of speech output, we
look at a particular application; a telephone enquiry service
for information retrieval.

You will not be surprised to learn, after the remarks on
graphics at the beginning of the previous chapter, that voice
input is at a much more rudimentary stage than voice output.
While moderately understandable speech can be synthesized
directly from text, the dream of a voice-operated typewriter
has yet to come true. Obviously the problem of coping with
different voices and accents is a difficult one, but there
are two much more serious stumbling-blocks. Firstly, it is
extremely hard to segment the acoustic wave into meaningful
units prior to recognition. People don't leave gaps between
words when they speak — you can check this by listening in
on a conversation in a foreign language which you don't
understand. Secondly, an enormous amount of knowledge about
the speaker, what he is likely to say, the situation, and the
world in general is used when understanding utterances. As
with pictures, perception presupposes understanding. The
final section of this chapter indicates what can be done at
present by way of voice input.

SPEECH STORAGE

Figure 5.2 shows an actual speech waveform for the
utterance "the price is ninety dollars and seventy-nine
cents". The first syllable is expanded and then expanded
again to show the fine detail. There is an enormous amount
of information in this waveform. Just how much depends on
the fidelity with which the signal needs to be reproduced.
The telephone system aims to transmit the frequency

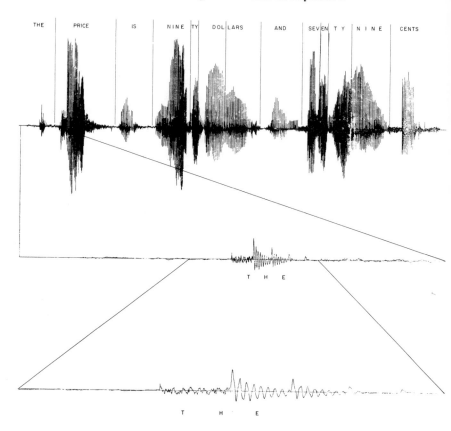

Figure 5.2 Waveform of the utterance "the price is 90 dollars
          and 79 cents"

components of speech between about 300 Hz and 3.5 kHz.
Actually, transmitting speech through the telephone system
degrades its quality very significantly, probably more than
you realize since everyone is so accustomed to telephone
speech. Try the dial-a-disk service and compare it with
high-fidelity music for a striking example of the kind of
degradation suffered.

     To digitize speech it must first be sampled in time and
then each sample changed to digital form with an A/D
converter (Figure 5.3). Thus a suitable sampling period and
the resolution for an individual sample both need to be
determined. It can be shown that the sampling frequency must
be at least twice the highest frequency of interest if the
original waveform is to be restorable from the digitized
version; in practice it needs to be slightly higher than this

and 8 - 10 kHz sampling is used for telephone-quality speech.
5- or 6-bit resolution is needed for each sample, leading to
a data-rate of around 50 Kbit/sec.

    This is quite a lot of data in computer storage terms. A
small main store of 8 Kbyte can only cope with a second of
speech, while a larger one of 128 Kbyte can hold 20 seconds.
A double-sided double-density floppy disk with 1.2 Mbyte can
hold slightly over 3 minutes, but the information must be
very carefully structured on the disk if it has to be read
off and replayed it in real time — although it is possible
with the assistance of DMA interfaces.

Predictive Encoding

    The scheme of digitizing samples directly is called PCM —
pulse-code modulation. It would seem that the data-rate
could be reduced by transmitting the difference between
successive samples instead of their absolute values: less
bits would be required for the difference signal for a given
overall accuracy because it does not assume such extreme
values as the absolute signal level. This is called DPCM —
differential PCM — and does reduce the data-rate slightly.
However, the improvement is not all that great, for the
speech wave has such sharp peaks on occasion that the
difference signal can be almost as large as the absolute
signal level.

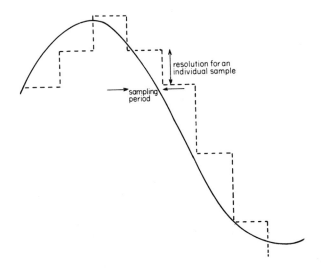

Figure 5.3 Digitizing a waveform

DPCM is a form of <u>predictive encoding</u>, in that the value
of the current sample is used to predict the next value and
only the difference between the actual and predicted values
is transmitted. Fairly recently, a much more sophisticated
predictive encoding scheme has been used extensively, where
the prediction is based on several sample values instead of
just one. Figure 5.4 illustrates how four samples can
predict the next one. The process can be thought of as
curve-fitting, where a curve is drawn through four points to
predict the position of the fifth. Only the prediction error
is actually transmitted.

Naturally the parameters of the curve which is fitted vary
as you pass along the speech waveform. The success of
predictive encoding is based on two facts:

   (1) the parameters vary relatively slowly;
and (2) if 10 points are fitted instead of the four of Figure
     5.4, the prediction error is very close to zero most
     of the time.

So-called LPC (linear predictive coding) schemes compute and
store the parameters of the predictive curve every 20 msec or
so, and store either the error signal or just the times when
it is significantly different from zero and its amplitude at
these times. The predictive curve has 10 parameters, and
curve-fitting is arranged so that the prediction is a linear
sum of the last 10 speech samples, weighted by these
parameters. This is why the encoding is called "linear".
Figure 5.5 shows a typical plot of the 10 parameters over a
1.25 second stretch of speech. It can be seen that they vary
quite slowly — much more slowly than the speech waveform of
Figure 5.2.

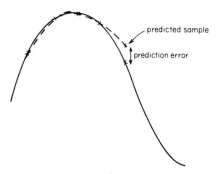

Figure 5.4 Predictive encoding based on four past sample
        values

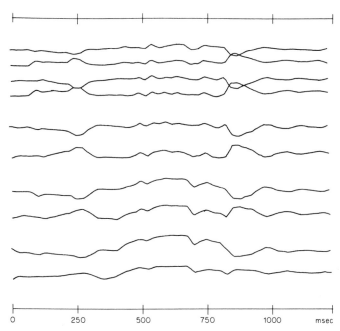

Figure 5.5 Linear predictive parameters for a sample of speech

The theory behind LPC is quite complicated, and this is no more than a brief introduction to the basic principle. Some further mathematical details appear in the Appendix to this chapter, and the references can be consulted for a more complete and balanced view. What matters most to us here is the data reduction achieved by the coding, and this is quite substantial. With 8-bit accuracy, the 10 prediction parameters occupy 4 Kbit/second if they are re-computed every 20 msec. The error signal, if just the non-zero samples are stored, will require about another 1 Kbit/second, so the total is 5 Kbit/second — only 10% of the storage required for PCM encoding. In fact this figure can be halved with more economical storage techniques, for some of the parameters require substantially less than 8 bits, and one standard for LPC based on a 22.5 msec interval between successive parameter sets uses only 2,400 bit/second. Then, an 8 Kbyte store can hold half a minute of speech, and a 1.2 Mbyte floppy disk over an hour.

Devices

Two low-cost devices for speech storage are available
commercially: one stores a speech waveform in a direct but
highly compressed form, and the other uses a single-chip
linear predictive system to regenerate speech from parameters
held in store.

A typical vocabulary for the first device is given in
Figure 5.6, which in fact is that of a talking pocket
calculator which has been around for some years. It contains
24 words. A different model with 64 words is marketed as a
computer output peripheral. This is about as much as can
reasonably be achieved with present read-only memory sizes,
although as technology improves a corresponding increase in
vocabulary can be expected. The speech quality is very poor,
at the limit of comprehension.

A single-chip linear predictor widens the scope
considerably. The task of regenerating speech from LPC
parameters is difficult, involving 20 multiplications and
additions per speech sample. Note that although a new set of
LPC parameters becomes available at 20 msec intervals, this
calculation must be repeated every speech sample — which at
an 8 kHz sampling rate is about one operation every 6 usec.
But it has been done, and the result, which is incorporated
into the Speak 'n Spell toy described in Chapter 1, holds
great promise for speech output from computers. With two 16
Kbyte read-only memory chips, this toy has a vocabulary of
nearly 300 words. The speech is rather worse than telephone
quality but nevertheless easily understandable, especially in
the context of an interactive man-machine system.

The process of encoding speech for either device is not an

oh	percent
one	low
two	over
three	root
four	em (m)
five	times
six	point
seven	overflow
eight	minus
nine	plus
times-minus	clear
equals	swap

Figure 5.6 Vocabulary of a talking calculator

easy one. Manufacturers provide their own vocabularies in read-only memory, and although a service is available for customized vocabularies it is expensive and involves substantial delay. Low-cost analysis systems can be expected in the future to allow a programmer to generate and fine-tune his own vocabulary, for the process of writing interactive programs will always involve a good deal of trial and error to get the dialogue just right. However, even if the equipment is available it is still not easy in practice to add new utterances to a voice response system using stored human speech, for one must assemble together special input hardware, a quiet room, a particular person so that the system has a consistent voice, and probably a dedicated computer. This discourages the application programmer from making cut-and-try attempts to render the man-machine dialogue as natural as possible in the final stages of debugging. The synthesis-from-phonetics technique described next means that he can change a speech message as easily as he could a VDU one, and evaluate its effect immediately.

SPEECH SYNTHESIS

People speak by using their vocal cords as a sound source, and making rapid gestures of the articulatory organs (lips, tongue, mouth, etc.). The resulting changes in shape of the vocal tract allow production of the different sounds that we know as the vowels and consonants of ordinary language. It is possible to simulate the action of the vocal tract electrically, and with the advent of cheap integrated circuits, simple, compact, and inexpensive synthesizers can be built without sacrificing the ability to produce the full range of speech sounds. To make the ever-changing patterns of speech, a synthesizer needs some form of continuously varying control, and just as there are many vocal tract organs involved simultaneously in speaking, so it is necessary to control several parameters of the synthesizer at once. Computer control is ideal for this. But before looking at the parameters which have to be controlled, we must learn something about human speech production.

The Anatomy of Speech

The so-called "voiced" sounds of speech — like the sound you make when you say "aaah" — are produced by passing air up from the lungs through the larynx or voicebox, which is

situated just behind the Adam's apple. The vocal tract from
the larynx to the lips acts as a resonant cavity, amplifying
certain frequencies and attenuating others.

The waveform generated by the larynx, however, is not
simply sinusoidal. (If it were, the vocal tract resonances
would merely give a sine wave of the same frequency but
amplified or attenuated according to how close it was to the
nearest resonance.) The larynx contains two folds of skin —
the vocal cords — which blow apart and flap together again
in each cycle of the pitch period. The pitch of a male voice
in speech varies from as low as 20 Hz to perhaps 250 Hz, with
a typical median value of 100 hz. For a female voice the
range is higher. The flapping action of the vocal cords
gives a waveform which can be approximated by the triangular
pulse of Figure 5.7. This has a rich spectrum of harmonics,
decaying at around 12 dB/octave, and each harmonic is
affected by the vocal tract resonances.

A simple model of the vocal tract is an organ-pipe-like
cylindrical tube (Figure 5.8), with a sound source at one end
(the larynx) and open at the other (the lips). This has
resonances at wavelengths 4L, 4L/3, 4L/5, ..., where L is the
length of the tube; and these correspond to frequencies c/4L,
3c/4L, 5c/4L, ... Hz, c being the speed of sound in air.
Calculating these frequencies, using a typical figure for the
distance between larynx and lips of 17 cm, and c=340 m/sec
for the speed of sound, leads to resonances at approximately
500 Hz, 1500 Hz, 2500 Hz, ...

When excited by the harmonic-rich waveform of the larynx,
the vocal tract resonances produce peaks known as <u>formants</u> in
the energy spectrum of the speech wave (Figure 5.9). The
lowest formant, called formant one, varies from around 200 Hz
to 1000 Hz during speech, the exact range depending on the
size of the vocal tract. Formant two varies from around 500
to 2500 Hz, and formant three from around 1500 to 3500 Hz.

Of course, speech is not a static phenomenon. The organ-
pipe model describes the speech spectrum during a

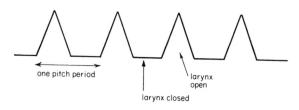

Figure 5.7 Approximate waveform produced by the larynx

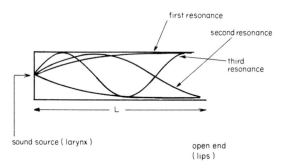

Figure 5.8 Resonances in the organ-pipe model of the vocal
            tract

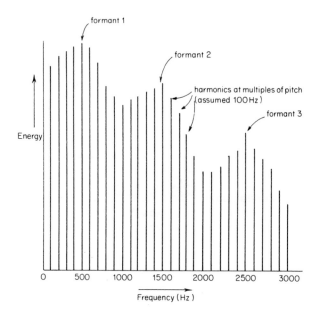

Figure 5.9 The energy spectrum of speech

continuously held vowel with the mouth in a neutral position
such as for "aaah". But in real speech the tongue and lips
are in continuous motion, altering the shape of the vocal
tract and hence the positions of the resonances. It is as if
the organ-pipe were being squeezed and expanded in different
places all the time. Say "ee" as in "heed" and notice how
close your tongue is to the roof of your mouth, causing a
constriction near the front of the vocal cavity.

    Linguists and speech engineers use a special frequency
analyser called a "sound spectrograph" to make a three-

dimensional plot of the variation of the speech energy
spectrum with time.   Figure 5.10 shows a spectrogram of the
utterance "go away". Frequency is given on the vertical
axis, and bands are shown at the beginning to indicate the
scale. Time is plotted horizontally, and energy is given by
the darkness of any particular area. The lower few formants
can be seen as dark bands extending horizontally, and they
are in continuous motion. Notice that in the neutral first
vowel of "away", the formant frequencies pass through
approximately the 500 Hz, 1500 Hz, and 2500 Hz that we
calculated earlier. (In fact, formants two and three are
somewhat lower than these values.) The fine vertical
striations in the spectrogram correspond to single openings
of the vocal cords. Of course, the pitch is continuously
changing throughout an utterance, and this can be seen on the
spectrogram by the differences in spacing of the striations.
Pitch change, or <u>intonation</u>, is singularly important in
lending naturalness to speech.

On a spectrogram, a continuously held vowel shows up as a
static energy spectrum. But beware — what we call a vowel
in everyday language is not the same thing as a "vowel" in
phonetic terms. Say "I" and feel how the tongue moves
continuously while you're speaking. Technically, this is a
<u>diphthong</u> or slide between two vowel positions, and not a
single vowel. And there are many more phonetically different
vowel sounds than the a, e, i, o, and u that we normally
think of. The words "hood" and "mood" have different vowels,
for example, as do "head" and "mead". The principal acoustic
difference between the various vowel sounds is in the
frequencies of the first two formants.

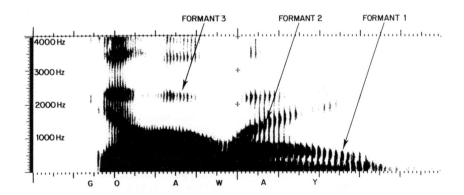

Figure 5.10 Spectrogram of the utterance "go away"

Speech involves other sounds, different from the voiced ones that we have been talking about up to now. When you whisper, the folds of the larynx are held slightly apart so that the air passing between them becomes turbulent, causing a noisy excitation of the resonant cavity. The formant peaks are still present, superimposed on the noise. Such "aspirated" sounds occur in the "h" of "hello", and for a very short time after the lips are opened at the beginning of "pit".

Constrictions made in the mouth produce hissy noises such as "ss", "sh", and "f". For example, in "ss" the tip of the tongue is high up, very close to the roof of the mouth. Turbulent air passing through this constriction causes a random noise excitation. For "sh", the tongue is flattened close to the roof of the mouth, in a position rather similar to that for "ee" but with a slightly narrower constriction, while "f" is produced with the upper teeth and lower lip. If the larynx is vibrating as well we get the corresponding voiced sounds "z", the "zh" in "azure", and "v". Because they are made near the front of the mouth, the resonances of the vocal tract have little effect on these hissy sounds. The complicated acoustic effects of noisy excitations in speech can be seen in the spectrogram below of "high altitude jets whizz past screaming".

Speech Synthesizers

In order to simulate electrically the resonating action of the vocal tract on the sound generated by the larynx, a waveform generator and several resonant filters in cascade are needed. Varying the frequency and amplitude of the sound source simulates changes in the pitch and loudness of the speech, and different vowels can be made by adjusting the positions of the resonances appropriately.

Although vocal tracts, like organ pipes, have an indefinite number of resonances, in practice only a few filters are employed in the chain. Most existing synthesizers simulate four or five formants, of which typically only the first three have controllable resonance positions. In fact, two formant filters are sufficient to generate most vowel-like speech sounds: a third is especially useful in distinguishing the "r" in "rice" from the "l" in "lice". Omitting the higher resonances means that a compensation filter needs to be introduced to give spectral lift at higher frequencies.

Whispery sounds can be synthesized by injecting noise,

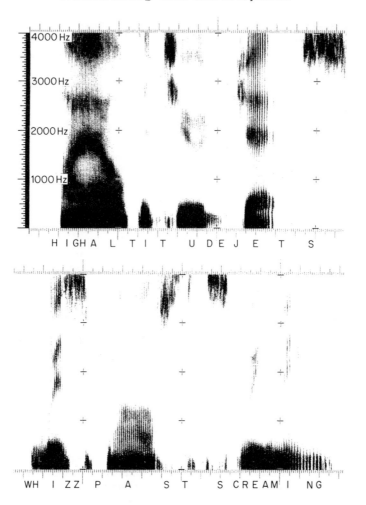

Figure 5.11 Spectrogram of "high-altitude jets whizz past
          screaming"

instead of the harmonic-rich pulse of the waveform generator,
into the chain of formant filters. For the sibilant sounds
produced at the front of the mouth, the noise should not be
injected into the formant chain, but instead passed through a
separate high-pass resonance whose centre frequency can be
controlled to give "f", "sh", and "ss".

These considerations lead to the block diagram of Figure
5.12. The eight arrows represent parameters of the system,
and if they are varied appropriately, it can be persuaded to
give a respectable imitation of almost any speech utterance.

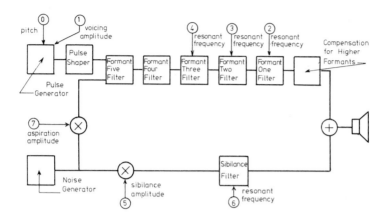

Figure 5.12 Block diagram of a resonance speech synthesizer

Storing Synthesizer Parameters

With 8 parameters stored as 6 bits each and updated every
20 msec (50 Hz), 2400 bits must be stored per second of
speech. Note that this is identical to the figure for the
LPC standard quoted in the previous section. The difference
between speech synthesis and LPC is that while automatic
techniques can be used to extract LPC parameters from live
utterances, the corresponding task for resonance synthesizers
cannot be so easily automated and invariably involves a good
deal of fine tuning. In one research laboratory a speech
synthesizer has been made to say "I enjoy the simple life, so
long as there's plenty of comfort" in a manner which is
indistinguishable to the untrained ear from the original
utterance, even under good listening conditions using high-
quality headphones — but the process of generating and
tuning the parameters took many months of a skilled person's
time! This is clearly out of the question for man-machine
communication applications.

SYNTHESIS FROM PHONEMES

The advantage of speech synthesis for man-computer
communication over LPC is that resonance parameters can be
generated from a phonetic transcription of the utterance.
Figure 5.13 gives the phonemes of British English. (In fact
linguists use an assortment of English letters, foreign
letters, and special symbols to describe utterances — these

uh	(the)	p	t	k	
a	(bud)	b	d	g	
e	(head)	m	n	ng	
i	(hid)				
o	(hod)	r	w	l	y
u	(hood)				
aa	(had)	s	z		
ee	(heed)	sh	zh		
er	(heard)	f	v		
uu	(food)	th	dh		
ar	(hard)	ch	j		
aw	(hoard)	h			

Figure 5.13 The phonemes of British English

are just a transliteration of our symbols.) Uh
f_uh_n_e_t_i_k t_r_aa_n_s_k_r_i_p_sh_uh_n i_z d_zh_a_s_t
uh "s_p_e_l_d uh_z s_p_uh_u_k_i_n" v_er_sh_uh_n uh_v
i_ng_g_l_i_sh. To generate speech from phonetics, a computer
program calculates a set of parameters describing the
resonances and excitation types which should be present in
the utterance, and sends these to a hardware speech
synthesizer like that of Figure 5.12.

The parameter tracks for "s_i_k_s" are shown as a set of
eight graphs in Figure 5.14. You can see the onset of the
hissy sound at the beginning and end (parameter 5), and the
amplitude of voicing (parameter 1) come on for the "i" and go
off again before the "k". The pitch (parameter 0) is falling
slowly throughout the utterance. These tracks are stylized:
they don't come from a human utterance. They were generated
from phonetics by a program.

"Speech-synthesis-by-rule" programs work from a table
which gives a standard set of parameters for each phoneme.
For example, part of the table for the vowels is shown in
Figure 5.15. Each one has the voicing amplitude set at the
same high value and the other, hissy, amplitudes zero. The
feature that distinguishes one vowel from another is just the
first two formant frequencies. The fundamental operation in
speech synthesis by rule is to extract the set of table
entries corresponding to each phoneme present in the
utterance, and interpolate between them to avoid sudden jumps
in the parameter values.

However, there are a host of exceptions to this. The
steady state of the "stop" sounds, b, d, g, p, t, and k is
actually silence! (Try saying a word like "butter" with a
very long t.) What distinguishes one from another are the
formant transitions just before and after the silent steady

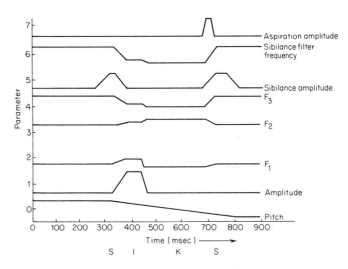

Figure 5.14 Parameter tracks for "s_i_k_s"

	voicing amplitude	formant one (Hz)	formant two (Hz)	formant three (Hz)
uh	max	490	1480	2500
a	max	720	1240	2540
e	max	560	1970	2640
i	max	360	2100	2700
o	max	600	890	2600
u	max	380	950	2440
aa	max	750	1750	2600
ee	max	290	2270	3090
er	max	580	1380	2440
ar	max	680	1080	2540
aw	max	450	740	2640
uu	max	310	940	2320

Figure 5.15 Synthesizer parameters for the vowels

state, and the burst of aspiration which occurs at the end of
the phoneme. This burst can be clearly seen at the release
of the "ĸ" in Figure 5.14. Another exception is that the "h"
phoneme does not have its own characteristic formant
frequencies but instead takes on the nature of the following
vowel, and is really just an aspirated extension of it. (Say
"who" and "he" slowly and deliberately, and examine the
configuration of your tongue, jaw and lips during the "h".)
The problem of speech synthesis by rule seems to be a matter
of getting all the small details just right.

  Speech synthesis from phonetics provides a convenient and
extremely economical representation of utterances for
storage. With about 40 phonemes requiring 6 bits each and a
normal speaking rate of 12 phonemes/second, the result is a
data-rate of only 70 bit/second. This is a factor of 700
less than PCM-encoded speech! A striking analogy can be
drawn with the representation of characters on a raster-
scanned screen by their indexes in a character-generating
read-only memory instead of storing the dot matrix for each
character as it occurs: for speech, the phoneme table in the
synthesis-by-rule program is the character generator, but the
process of joining phonemes together is much more complicated
than placing characters side by side.

  Apart from phenomenal storage efficiency, there are other
advantages in storing phonetics and synthesizing speech in
real time over the more conventional methods of handling
encoded versions of natural speech, especially from the point
of view of system development and maintenance. The
utterances can be stored as phonetic text incorporated into
the particular parts of the program where they are used.
Thus, given adequate software and hardware organization,
output requires only a "speak" command which takes a short
character-string as argument — exactly the same as VDU
output. Dialogues can be modified immediately without the
need to set up a recording session. One inconvenience is
that application programmers must acquire skill in phonetic
transcription. Fortunately, an interactive situation in
which the effects of modifications to the transcription can
be heard immediately provides an ideal environment in which
to learn this art.

  The main drawback to the use of speech synthesis from
phonetics is the poor quality of the output. Current systems
produce speech which is intelligible in short stretches but
rather difficult to listen to for long periods. However, the
quality of articulation is continually being improved as
research by acoustic phoneticians uncover new facts about the
structure of speech. The biggest problem is in controlling

the attitudinal and emphatic aspects of the speech: these
are "hidden features" of which we are not normally aware but
nevertheless are vital to the effective communication of
information. Lack of attention to prosody is the chief
reason why much current synthetic speech sounds strained and
unnatural, and we examine this next.

RHYTHM AND INTONATION

   Phoneticians divide features of natural speech into
segmental ones (giving segments of syllables) and
suprasegmental ones (relating to the prosody of the
utterance), and this distinction is useful in synthesis work
as well. Of course, segmental synthesis must come first,
otherwise there is no vehicle to carry the prosodic features.
However, comparatively little consideration has been given to
methods for suprasegmental synthesis which provide enough
freedom to allow production of natural-sounding speech.
   Suprasegmental features can be split into two basic
categories: features of voice quality and features of voice
dynamics. Variations in voice quality — which are accounted
for by anatomical differences between speakers and long-term
muscular idiosyncracies — have little part to play in man-
machine communication, so only elements of the second
category are considered here. These are:

   rhythm
   intonation (pitch fluctuation)
   pauses
   speed of speaking
   mean pitch level
   range between highest and lowest pitch levels
   loudness.

Rhythm

   The easiest way to control the timing of speech
synthesized by rule is to store a standard duration for each
phoneme in the rule table. Unfortunately, this does not
produce acceptable-sounding speech, for in reality the
duration of a particular phoneme depends partly on its
environment: whether the phoneme forms part of a stressed
syllable, whether it is word-final, and so on. This can be
taken into account by having the person who provides the
phonetic transcription annotate it with phoneme durations,

but although it is often done in practice this is not really
an acceptable solution for man-computer communication
purposes because it needs a considerable amount of specialist
knowledge and a great deal of trial and error.

There are two approaches to automatic assignment of
duration, neither of which have yet produced really
satisfactory results. One is to use the syntactic structure
of the utterance — the pattern of clauses, phrases, and
nouns, verbs and other word classes within phrases — as a
basis for rhythm. Either the syntax of the utterance must be
specified with its phonetic transcription, or it must be
deduced by a syntax analysis program. Then a host of rules
is used to give the duration of each phoneme from its context
and the role its parent word plays in the syntax.

The second method of duration assignment is based on
theories of rhythm which derive from the metric analysis of
poetry. Stress points are marked in the phonetic input, and
the program juggles with phoneme durations to balance the
times between the stresses, for there seems to be general
agreement between phoneticians that there is a tendency for
stress points to be equally spaced in time. More subtle
points like the rhythm of different patterns of syllables are
sometimes taken into account as well.

Intonation

Pitch is another feature that must be controlled by a
synthesis program. Again, pitch level for each phoneme may
be provided with the phonetic transcription, but this places
an unreasonable burden on the person who generates the
transcriptions.

Theories of British English intonation invariably segment
utterances into units called "tone groups", each with a
single salient or "tonic" syllable (and a number of other
syllables). One classification of intonation identifies five
different primary pitch contours, each hinging on the tonic
syllable. Several secondary contours, which are variations
on the primary ones, are defined as well. If the tonic
syllable and desired contour type are specified with each
utterance, the standard contours can be retrieved from
storage and fitted to utterances before synthesis.

Other Features

The remaining suprasegmental features are not so difficult

to deal with in a conversational speech output system. To a
small extent, intelligibility can be traded for speed of
speaking, and long-term variations in tempo can allow
experienced operators the convenience of more rapid
conversation, deliberate speech being reserved for novices.
Similarly, a sophisticated system could perhaps use small
increases in pitch range to lend a dramatic note to certain
utterances, as, for example, when a user asks more than once
for a message to be repeated. It is sometimes useful to have
different voices available (for example, male and female),
but apart from this the mean pitch level need not be varied
at all. Similarly, there is little reason to alter the
overall loudness (contrary to intuition, loudness is a very
weak clue to stress, and is outshadowed by rhythm and
intonation). Pauses are a rather more difficult matter which
can depend on the syntactic structure of the utterance, but
they can be controlled satisfactorily by associating a few
different pause durations with punctuation marks in the input
and allowing the person giving the phonetic transcription to
use them as he thinks fit.

Communicating Utterances to the Synthesis Program

Here are examples of the way utterances are specified to a
speech synthesis system which has been developed in one
research laboratory.

```
3 ^ aw t uh/m aa t i k  /s i n th uh s i s  uh v
/*s p ee t sh, 1 ^ f r uh m  uh  f uh/*n e t i k
/r e p r uh z e n/t e i sh uh n.
```

The standard phonetic symbols are coded into one or two
letters, as in Figure 5.13, to cope with the normal
limitations of computer input devices. Slashes mark the
stressed syllables, and an asterisk identifies the point of
tonic stress of an intonation pattern. Utterances are
divided by punctuation marks into tone groups, and the shape
of the intonation contour is specified by a numeral at the
start of each one. Crude control over pauses is achieved by
punctuation marks: full stop, for example, signals a pause
while a comma does not. The "^" character stands for a
"silent stress" or breath point.

READING ORDINARY TEXT

So far we have looked at synthesizing speech by rule from a phonetic description. However, if ordinary text could be used as input new applications would appear, for any text stored in a computer system could be read, and not just phonetic utterances which are entered expressly for the purpose of speech output. In fact there is already on the market a machine which reads aloud ordinary books. This not only implements speech synthesis from text but also deals with the problem of optical character recognition. The speech it produces is really very poor, but it is used daily by blind people who of course have a very great incentive to learn to recognize its voice.

What are the problems in speech synthesis from text? There are two: first the text must be translated into phonetics, and second the suprasegmental information which is needed to control the synthesizer must be gleaned automatically. These tasks interact, particularly in the area of rhythm, for timing and pronunciation are closely intertwined. The first problem is the easier. A great deal can be done with simple letter-to-sound rules, which specify phonetic equivalents of word fragments and single letters. The longest stored fragment which matches the current word is translated, and then the same strategy is adopted on the remainder of the word. Figure 5.16 shows some English fragments and their pronunciations.

Special action has to be taken with final "e"'s. These lengthen the preceding vowel, so that "bit" becomes "bite" and so on. Unfortunately, if the word has a suffix the "e" must be detected even though it is no longer final, as in "lonely", and it is even dropped sometimes ("biting"). To make matters worse the suffix may be another word: "kiteflying". Although simple procedures can be developed to take care of common word endings like "-ly", "-ness", "-d"; it is difficult to decompose compound words like "wisecrack" and "bumblebee" reliably. And there are exceptions to the final "e" rule ("epitome", "macrame").

The rhythm of a word depends on its decomposition into prefixes and suffixes. For example, "diplomat", "diplomacy", and "diplomatic" each have stress on a different syllable! Prefixes usually bear the stress if the word is a noun but not if it is a verb — "extract" is an example. Notice that the word "prefix" itself is a counterexample; most people say it with stress on the "pre" even as a verb. The syntactic part of speech of a word has other effects. For example, "approximate" is pronounced differently depending on whether

fragment	pronunciation
-p-	p
-ph-	f
-phe¦	f_ee
-phe¦s	f_ee_z
-phot-	f_uh_u_t
-place¦-	p_l_e_i_s
-plac¦i-	p_l_e_i_s_i
-ple¦ment-	p_l_i_m_e_n_t
-plie¦-	p_l_aa_i_y
-post	p_uh_u_s_t
-pp-	p
-pp¦ly-	p_l_ee
-preciou-	p_r_e_s_uh
-proce¦d-	p_r_uh_u_s_ee_d
-prope¦r-	p_r_o_p_uh_r
-prov-	p_r_uu_v
-purpose-	p_er_p_uh_s
-push-	p_u_sh
-put	p_u_t
-puts	p_u_t_s

Note: "-" means that other fragments can proceed or
       follow this one in a word.
       "¦" is used to separate suffices, and is placed
       after a point where a silent "e" is deemed to
       occur.

Figure 5.16 Word fragments and their pronunciations

it is an adjective or a verb, and "house" depends on whether
it is a noun or a verb. "Wind" has two pronunciations, one
of them only is used as a noun (nowadays, although it used to
be different), but both are verbs (to wind somebody, or to
wind them round your little finger)! Here, it is clearly
necessary to take semantics into account as well as syntax.
There are other example of semantic distinctions, although
they are fairly uncommon. "Unionized" can be pronounced in
two ways (un-ionized and union-ized), and the "lead" is
different in "red lead" and "dog lead". Figure 5.17
illustrates the four major influences on pronunciation and
rhythm that we have discussed, with some examples.
    Deriving intonation from text is a very difficult matter.
To read aloud you really have to understand what you're
saying. For example, pitch often — but by no means always

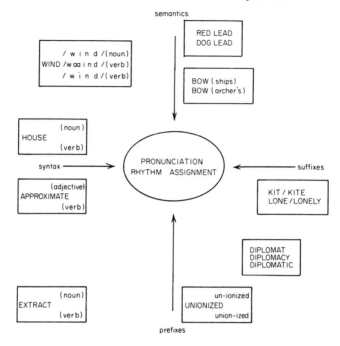

Figure 5.17 The major influences on pronunciation and rhythm

— rises on a question, the extent and abruptness of the rise
depending on factors like whether a proper information-
bearing reply or merely confirmation is expected. A
distinctive pitch pattern accompanies the introduction of a
new topic. The placement of tonic stress highlights new
information, and can be used to bring out contrasts as in

"He didn't have a RED car, he had a BLACK one".

In general, the intonation patterns used by a reader depend
not only on the text itself, but on his interpretation of it
and also on his expectation of the listener's reaction to it.
For example,

"He had a RED car" (I think you thought it was black),
"He had a red BIcycle" (I think you thought it was a car).

These subtleties are really very difficult to incorporate
into a computer program.

A TELEPHONE ENQUIRY SERVICE

Let's look at a computer system which allows interactive
information retrieval from an ordinary touch-tone telephone.
The caller employs the touch-tone keypad shown in Figure 5.18
for input, and the computer generates a synthetic voice
response. Figure 5.19 shows the process of making contact
with the system.

Advantage is taken of the disparate speeds of input
(keyboard) and output (speech) to hasten the dialogue by
imposing a question-answer structure on it, with the computer
taking the initiative. The machine can afford to be slightly
verbose if by so doing it makes the caller's response easier,
and therefore more rapid. Moreover, operators who are
experienced enough with the system to anticipate questions
can easily forestall them just by typing ahead.

An important aim of the system is to allow application
programmers with no special knowledge of speech to write
independent services for it. Figure 5.20 shows an example of
the use of one such application program, the Stores
Information Service.

A distinction is drawn throughout the system between data
entries and commands, the latter being prefixed by a "*". In
this example, the programmer chose to define a command for
each possible question about a component, so that a new
component name can be entered at any time without ambiguity.
The price paid for the resulting brevity of dialogue is the
burden of memorizing the meaning of the commands. This is an

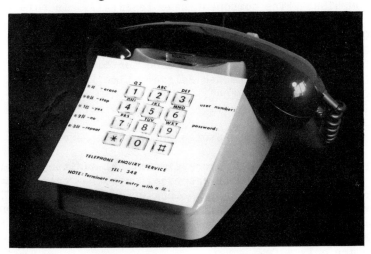

Figure 5.18 A touch-tone telephone terminal

```
CALLER:    Dials the service.
COMPUTER:  Answers telephone.  "Hello, Telephone Enquiry
           Service.  Please enter your user number".
CALLER:    Enters user number.
COMPUTER:  "Please enter your password".
CALLER:    Enters password.
COMPUTER:  Checks validity of password.  If invalid, the
           user is asked to re-enter his user number.
           Otherwise, "Which service do you require?"
CALLER:    Enters service number.
```

Figure 5.19 Making contact with the telephone enquiry system

```
COMPUTER:  "Stores Information Service.  Please enter
           component name".
CALLER:    Enters "SN7406#".
COMPUTER:  "The component name is SN7406.  Is this
           correct?"
CALLER:    Enters "*1#" (system convention for "yes").
COMPUTER:  "This component is in stores".
CALLER:    Enters "*7#" (command for "price").
COMPUTER:  "The component price is 35 pence".
CALLER:    Enters "*8#" (command for "minimum number").
COMPUTER:  "The minimum number of this component kept in
           stores is 10".
CALLER:    Enters "SN7417#".
COMPUTER:  "The component name is SN7417.  Is this
           correct?"
CALLER:    Enters "*1#".
COMPUTER:  "This component is not in stores".
CALLER:    Enters "*9#" (command for "delivery time").
COMPUTER:  "The expected delivery time is 14 days".
CALLER:    Enters "*0#".
COMPUTER:  "Which service do you require?"
```

Figure 5.20 The Stores Information Service

inherent disadvantage of a one-dimensional auditory display
over the more conventional graphical output: presenting
menus by speech is tedious and long-winded. In practice,
however, for a simple task such as the Stores Information
Service it is quite convenient for the caller to search for
the appropriate command by trying out all possibilities —
there are only a few.

The problem of memorizing commands is alleviated by

establishing some system-wide conventions. Each input is
terminated by a "#", and the meaning of standard commands is
given in Figure 5.21.

A summary of services available on the system is given in
Figure 5.22. A priority structure is imposed upon them, with
higher service numbers being available only to higher
priority users. Services in the lowest range (1-99) can be
obtained by all, while those in the highest range (900-999)
are maintenance services, available only to the system
designers. Access to the lower-numbered "games" services can
be inhibited by a priority user — this was found necessary
to prevent over-use of the system! Another advantage of
telephone access to an information retrieval system is that
some day-to-day maintenance can be done remotely, from the
office telephone.

VOICE INPUT

Most existing voice input systems are limited to
discrimination between words spoken in isolation.
Recognizing connected speech involves much more than this,
for, as noted earlier, people don't normally leave gaps
between words when they speak. For many applications,
isolated-word identification is quite sufficient. For
example, the capability of distinguishing 12 words
representing touch-tone telephone keys would considerably
enhance the telephone enquiry service described above.

There is an obvious trade-off between recognition
performance, vocabulary size, number of users, and whether
the machine has an opportunity to calibrate speakers' voices
in a training session. Typical systems can recognize a small
vocabulary like the digits with high accuracy, even with a
large number of completely unknown speakers. For bigger

*#	-	Erase this input line, regardless of what has been typed before the "*".
*0#	-	Stop. Used to exit from any service.
*1#	-	Yes.
*2#	-	No.
*3#	-	Repeat question or summarize state of current transaction.
# alone	-	Short form of repeat. Repeats or summarizes in an abbreviated fashion.

Figure 5.21 System-wide conventions for the service

```
1  -  tells the time
2  -  Biffo (a game of NIM)
3  -  MOO (a game similar to that marketed under the
      name "Mastermind")
4  -  error demonstration
5  -  speak a file in phonetic format
6  -  listening test
7  -  music (allows you to enter a tune and play it)
8  -  gives the date

101 - stores information service
102 - computes means and standard deviations
103 - telephone directory

411 - user information
412 - change password
413 - gripe (permits feedback on services from caller)

600 - first year laboratory marks entering service

910 - repeat utterance (allows testing of system)
911 - speak utterance (allows testing of system)
912 - enable/disable user 100 (a no-password guest user
      number)
913 - mount a magnetic tape on the computer
914 - set/reset demonstration mode (prohibits access by
      low-priority users)
915 - inhibit games
916 - inhibit the MOO game
917 - disable password checking when users log in
```

Figure 5.22 Summary of services on a telephone enquiry system

vocabularies, however, a training session is needed for reasonable performance. It should be emphasized that the user is training the machine to recognize his voice rather than being trained to speak in the right way! — but some adaptation to the machine inevitably takes place. Training usually consists of saying a small number of samples of each word, which are stored and used as a basis for subsequent matching by the machine. Figure 5.23 summarizes some typical performances of word recognizers.

One commercial word recognizer is being used in a variety of applications. One example is routing luggage at an airport. The operator picks up a bag and places it on a conveyer, reading the destination on the label to the machine. The bag is then sent automatically to the

vocabulary size	number of speakers	recognition accuracy
without training		
10	30	98 %
100	4	92.5 %
with training		
10	10	99.8 %
34	12	98.5 %
54	2	97 %
200	1	96 %

Figure 5.23 Typical word-recognition scores

appropriate loading bay. The advantage of voice input here
is that it leaves the operator free to handle the luggage
without having to press keys. However, the word recognizer
must cope with extraneous noises, which occur even though
close-fitting noise-cancelling microphones are used, breath
noise, and remarks not intended for it which the operator
inevitably makes to his colleagues. Destinations are
presented on a VDU which the operator checks to ensure that
recognition is correct.

The number of words in the vocabulary of a speech
recognition task is not so much a limitation as is the number
of different words that can be said at any given point in the
dialogue — the "branching factor". For example, a speech
recognizer may be able to distinguish the colours ("red",
"green", "blue", ...) and also the digits ("zero", "one",
"two", ...), but may confuse some colours with some digits.
(perhaps "green" and "nine", "blue" and "two", "yellow" and
"seven"). This need not cause ambiguity if the dialogue is
structured so that digits and colours are never expected at
the same time. The speaker might say "colour: yellow;
quantity: seven" and provided the recognizer can tell the
word "colour" from the word "quantity" it need not be able to
discriminate the names of the colours from the digits.

Connected speech recognition is limited to highly
constrained situations which allow a great deal to be
predicted about what is likely to be said. One project used

a chess-playing task where the user spoke his moves to the
machine. It incorporated knowledge of the vocabulary of
chess moves, legal moves in the current board position, and
even which moves it figured were the most likely. It is
rumoured that if you just coughed into the microphone the
machine, unable to recognize anything, would assume that you
had made what it thought was the best move in that situation
and play it for you!

It is important to distinguish the problem of spotting
known words in continuous speech from recognizing an
utterance assuming that it is formed from known words. Word
spotting requires an absolute judgement of whether the word
or words appeared or not, while if one can assume that just
known words are spoken it is only necessary to balance
possible interpretations and decide which is most likely — a
rather easier task. A commercial device for continuous
speech recognition has recently been marketed by a Japanese
firm (it's expensive — around 35,000 pounds at the time of
writing), but it assumes that all input is "legal". Word
spotting is more difficult, but much more useful, for "er's",
"um's", and asides not intended for the recognizer can all be
rejected. Some progress has been made on this problem in
research laboratories.

SUMMARY

There is almost a continuum of speech output devices, from
the homely tape recorder to machines which read printed text
aloud. The speech quality ranges along this continuum from
excellent to barely understandable, while the flexibility and
convenience for use in interactive systems decreases in the
other direction.

Direct storage of unencoded digital speech requires a high
data-rate, which makes it costly because mechanical recording
media like disks are needed even for short stretches of
speech. The recent introduction of LPC provides a way of
reducing the data-rate at the expense of much more complex
output equipment, but this disadvantage is considerably
lessened by the availability of single-chip LPC decoders.
However, storing speech in LPC form still presents problems,
partly because of the complexity of the encoding process but
more importantly because any live recording takes time and
organization to set up and this discourages final adjustments
of synthetic responses for maximum effectiveness. The
quality of LPC stored speech is fairly high.

Speech synthesis from a written representation provides an

extremely economical storage method. Again a hardware
synthesizer is required, but the cost is not great. Speech
can be generated from phonetics, lightly sprinkled with
markers to indicate the rhythmic beats in the utterance, and
the intonation contour. However, the speech quality is poor.
First-time listeners often understand under half of what is
said, although in an interactive situation where the context
heavily constrains what can be said, they understand much
more, and they improve rapidly with experience. The
deficiencies in speech synthesized by rule stem partly from
weak articulation and partly from the difficulty of
specifying the features of rhythm and intonation. It seems
that the articulation will be improved by a process of
getting the details right, and steady progress is being made.
Rhythm and intonation are rather different, however, because
although the phonetic transcription provides a standard way
of specifying what is to be said, there is no such standard
notation for specifying how it is to be said. Nevertheless,
speech synthesis from phonetics has the important advantage
over stored speech in man-machine systems that the programmer
can more easily tailor his utterances to provide a natural
dialogue, and we can expect to find it being used more and
more.

Synthesis from text presents even more difficult problems,
for in order to read aloud you have to understand what you're
reading and also to some extent predict your listener's
reaction to it. Although systems for reading aloud do exist
and are used by blind people, the quality of output is so low
that considerable practice and persistence are needed to
understand them. Because of the low quality output, the
principal advantage gained from using unadorned text as
input, namely that any document which happens to be stored in
a computer system can be read, does not justify its use in
man-machine dialogues which have to be programmed specially
anyway.

Having looked at the telephone enquiry service as an
example of what can be done with simple speech output, we can
weigh up some of the pros and cons of the medium. The chief
advantage is that any touch-tone telephone can become a
computer terminal, and a ready-made distribution network
exists. Set against this is the fact that speech is
ephemeral: if you miss it, it's gone and there's no chance
of re-reading it as with text on a VDU. It is important to
avoid the absurd situation of copying computer utterances
down on paper by hand.

Finally, although it still has a long way to go, speech
output is far more advanced than speech input. One

commercial word recognizer on the market can cope with a
vocabulary of several dozen isolated words, although there is
naturally a trade-off between recognition accuracy and
vocabulary size. It requires training with each person who
uses it. Continuous speech recognition is still a difficult
research problem, although progress has been made using
constrained dialogues.

FURTHER READING

Ainsworth, W.A. (1976) "Mechanisms of Speech Recognition."
    Pergamon, Oxford.
        A nice, easy-going introduction to speech
        recognition, this book covers the acoustic
        structure of the speech signal in a way which
        makes it useful as background reading for speech
        synthesis, as well.

Flanagan, J.L. (1972) "Speech Analysis, Synthesis and
    Perception." Springer-Verlag, Berlin.
        This book is the speech researcher's bible, and
        like the bible, it's not all that easy to read.
        I'd recommend you to start on something else —
        say Ainsworth or Holmes — and just use Flanagan
        as a reference when you want to check on a
        specific fact or theory.

Flanagan, J.L. and Rabiner, L.R. (1973) "Speech Synthesis."
    Dowden, Hutchinson & Ross, Stroudsburg, Pennsylvania.
        This is a collection of previously-published
        research papers on speech synthesis, rather than
        a unified book. It contains most of the classic
        papers on the subject from 1940 - 1972, and is a
        very useful reference work.

Holmes, J.N. (1972) "Speech Synthesis." Mills and Boom,
    London.
        This little book, by one of Britain's foremost
        workers in the field, introduces the subject of
        speech synthesis and speech synthesizers.

Ladefoged, P. (1975) "A Course in Phonetics." Harcourt Brace
    Johanovich, New York.
        If you want to find out more about speech
        synthesis, you'll have to learn something about
        phonetics. Ladefoged's book is a delightful,

easy-to-read introductory text on the subject,
full of helpful and instructive experiments and
exercises that you can do yourself.

Markel, J.D. and Gray, A.H. (1976) "Linear Prediction of
Speech." Springer-Verlag, Berlin.
This is an exhaustive (and exhausting!) treatment
of linear predictive analysis and coding.
Although the development is largely theoretical,
Fortran programs are given for parts of the
coding and decoding processes.

Rabiner, L.R. and Schafer, R.W. (1978) "Digital Processing of
Speech Signals." Prentice-Hall, Englewood Cliffs, New
Jersey.
A comprehensive text on digital signal processing
for speech, this covers all sorts of analysis
techniques including linear prediction. From the
point of view of the present book, it's a
compendium on speech storage, and does not tackle
any of the higher-level problems of speech
synthesis — like articulation, rhythm,
intonation, or pronunciation.

APPENDIX: LINEAR PREDICTION OF SPEECH

The basic idea of linear predictive coding is as follows.
We have a sampled signal x_n (n = 0,1,2,...) that is to be
transmitted through a low-capacity channel. Instead of
digitizing and transmitting the samples directly, we compute
predicted values of them according to the formula

$$x_n^* = a_1 x_{n-1} + a_2 x_{n-2} \cdots + a_p x_{n-p}$$

and transmit the difference between the actual and predicted
values,

$$e_n = x_n - x_n^*,$$

at each stage. The a's are numbers which we will see how to
determine shortly, and there are p of them — p is usually
around 10 for speech coding. At the receiving end, the
original value x_n can be reconstituted from the prediction
error e_n and the numbers $a_1, \ldots, a_p$ by

$$x_n = e_n + a_1 x_{n-1} + a_2 x_{n-2} \cdots + a_p x_{n-p}.$$

This scheme may result in compression of data if the a's change relatively slowly — they must be transmitted from time to time but not as often as every sample of x — and if x_n^* is a good prediction of x_n, so that the error signal e_n requires substantially less bits than x_n. It is necessary to ensure that the error signal is small, and this is done by choosing appropriate values for the a's. Let's minimize the total squared prediction error

$$M = \sum_n e_n^2$$

by choice of the a's. This minimization will be done repeatedly, usually every 20 msec or so. Speech samples are taken every 100 usec (10 kHz sampling rate), and so 200 samples elapse between successive minimizations. Transmitting the 10 coefficient values every 200 samples occupies only a small fraction of the channel which would be required to transmit each x_n, and we stand to gain substantially if the error signal can be made small. The number of error samples which need to contribute to M will be considered in a moment.

The total squared prediction error is

$$M = \sum_n e_n^2 = \sum_n [x_n - \sum_{k=1}^{p} a_k x_{n-k}]^2 .$$

Minimize this by choosing the coefficients a_j to make the derivatives zero:

$$\frac{dM}{da_j} = -2 \sum_n x_{n-j}[x_n - \sum_{k=1}^{p} a_k x_{n-k}] = 0,$$

so $\sum_{k=1}^{p} a_k \sum_n x_{n-j} x_{n-k} = \sum_n x_n x_{n-j}$ $j = 1, 2, \ldots, p.$

What about the range of the n-summation? It seems reasonable to use a fixed number of elements, say N, starting at h, to estimate the prediction coefficients between sample number h and sample number h+N. This leads to

$$\sum_{k=1}^{p} a_k Q_{jk}^h = Q_{0j}^h \qquad j = 1, 2, \ldots, p,$$

where $Q_{jk}^h = \sum_{n=h}^{h+N-1} x_{n-j} x_{n-k} .$

Now

$$Q_{jk}^h = Q_{kj}^h,$$

so we have a diagonally symmetric matrix equation. The a's can be found by inverting the Q-matrix. In fact, the formidable problem of matrix inversion is substantially easier for diagonally symmetric matrices, because a special theorem (Cholesky's theorem) can be used which leads to an efficient procedure for solving the matrix equation. This method of computing the prediction coefficients has become known as the <u>covariance</u> <u>method</u>.

Before specifying the range of summation, our matrix equation had coefficients

$$\sum_n x_{n-j} x_{n-k}.$$

Now if a doubly infinite summation is made, with x_n being defined as 0 whenever $n < 0$, we can make use of the fact that

$$\sum_{n=-\infty}^{\infty} x_{n-j} x_{n-k} = \sum_{n=-\infty}^{\infty} x_{n-j+1} x_{n-k+1}$$

$$= \ldots = \sum_{n=-\infty}^{\infty} x_n x_{n+j-k}$$

to simplify the matrix equation into the form

$$R_0 a_1 + R_1 a_2 + R_2 a_3 + \ldots = R_1$$

$$R_1 a_1 + R_0 a_2 + R_1 a_3 + \ldots = R_2$$

$$R_2 a_1 + R_1 a_2 + R_0 a_3 + \ldots = R_3$$

$$\cdot \quad \cdot \quad \cdot$$

where
$$R_m = \sum_n x_n x_{n+m} \qquad m = 0,1,\ldots,p.$$

An elegant method for solving this special system of equations exists which requires much less computational effort than even Cholesky decomposition.

Of course, it is impractical to compute these infinite sums — and undesirable when the frequency spectrum of the signal is changing — so a windowing procedure

$$x_n' = w_n x_n$$

is used to reduce the signal to zero outside a finite range of interest. A suitable window shape for n terms is sketched

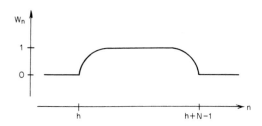

Figure 5.24 A window shape for the autocorrelation method

N	Autocorrelation		Covariance	
	multiplications/ divisions	additions/ subtractions	multiplications/ divisions	additions/ subtractions
100			1465	1540
200	2520	2300		

Table 5.1 Computational requirements of linear predictive
         analysis

in Figure 5.24.   Then we define

$$R_m^h = \sum_{n=h}^{h+N-1} x_n' x_{n+m}' \qquad m = 0,1,\ldots,p.$$

Note that no values outside the range $h \le n < h+N$ are
required, since the windowing function is zero there.

This is known as the <u>autocorrelation</u> <u>method</u> of computing
prediction coefficients.   The autocorrelation method needs a
larger value of N to achieve the same degree of accuracy as
the covariance method; typically 200 samples in speech
applications as opposed to 100.

Table 5.1 compares the amount of computation needed using
the autocorrelation and covariance methods.   Although the
autocorrelation method requires more arithmetic than the
covariance method, it does have advantages to compensate, for
its numerical stability is much greater.   In either case the
whole procedure must be repeated every 20 msec, so you can
see that linear predictive speech analysis involves a great
deal of rapid number-crunching.

Subject Index